Cicerone
County Walking Series

WALKING IN WORCESTERSHIRE

*A tight squeeze on the
Worcester & Birmingham Canal - Astwood Lock*

WALKING IN WORCESTERSHIRE

An explorer's guide to towns, villages
and the countryside

by

David Hunter

CICERONE PRESS
MILNTHORPE, CUMBRIA

© D. Hunter 1999
ISBN 1 85284 286 5
A catalogue record for this book is available from the British Library.

Text: David Hunter
Sketch Maps and input at all stages: Vera Hunter
Photography: David and Vera Hunter

OTHER BOOKS IN THIS SERIES

Walking in Cheshire
Walking in Cornwall
Walking in Devon
Walking in Dorset
Walking in County Durham
Walking in Kent (2 vols)

Walking in Lancashire
Walking in Northumberland
Walking in Oxfordshire
Walking in Somerset
Walking in Warwickshire

OTHER CICERONE GUIDES BY THE SAME AUTHOR

The Shropshire Hills
Walking Down the Wye

Walking Offa's Dyke Path
Severn Walks

Front Cover: Habberley Valley

CONTENTS

(Note all distances quoted are approximate)

IMPORTANT
MAP UPDATE INFORMATION

The Ordnance Survey are gradually replacing the 1.25000 Pathfinder Series with new Explorer Maps covering much greater areas. Where available this information has been included. Please see note MAPS in the Introduction for further information.

DIAGRAM OF ACCESS ROADS

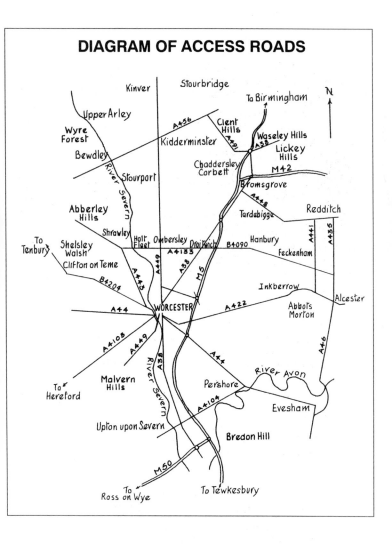

The Canal Basin, Stourport

Advice to Readers

Readers are advised that whilst every effort is taken by the author to ensure the accuracy of this guidebook, changes can occur which may affect the contents. It is advisable to check locally on transport, accommodation, shops etc but even rights-of-way can be altered.

The publisher would welcome notes of any such changes

COUNTRY CODE

Please observe this whenever you are walking in the countryside.

- Enjoy the countryside and respect its life and work
- Guard against all risk of fire
- Take your litter home
- Fasten all gates
- Help to keep all water clean
- Keep your dogs under control
- Protect wildlife, plants and trees
- Keep to public paths across farmland
- Take special care on country roads
- Leave livestock, crops and machinery alone
- Make no unnecessary noise
- Use gates and stiles to cross fences, hedges and walls

1
Introduction

WORCESTERSHIRE has a varied landscape but few would think of it as a mountainous region. Let me reassure those hillwalkers, who may feel they have been given short measure if an outing does not provide at least one high viewpoint, that there are many worthwhile hills to be climbed.

In the north the high ground includes the Clent, Waseley and Lickey Hills with points over the magic thousand feet. Not particularly impressive, until it is pointed out that in one direction there is nothing higher between this piece of middle England and the Ural mountains. To the west the Abberley and Woodberry Hills top 900 feet. In the south-east, Broadway Hill had the reputation of giving a view to fourteen counties from its lofty 1026 feet. The great whale-backed Bredon Hill (961 feet), where A. E. Housman strayed from the strict geography of the Shropshire Lad to look over "the coloured counties", provides panoramic views that are not bettered by some peaks of greater stature. Finally there are the incomparable Malvern Hills, an easily accessed paradise for walkers of all ages and abilities. From here join John Evelyn, the seventeenth century diarist, in his enjoyment of "One of the goodliest vistas in England". The Worcestershire Beacon, where fires were set on "Malvern's lonely height" to warn of the approach of the Spanish Armada tops out at 1394 feet; nearby North Hill is only a little lower. The Herefordshire Beacon (1108 feet), where Iron Age man established an extensive hill fort, one of the finest in the country, is the place from which to look up the switchback of successive peaks and out to many distant, inviting hills or down to the mosaic patterns of the Severn plain.

Before moving on it is time to frame the picture and set it in the context of the wider world. An unnecessary exercise for those who live here but I do not forget the enquiries of my colleagues when I, a born and bred Londoner, was about to depart for my now adopted county: "Worcester - where's that? Somewhere near Wales isn't it?"

To the north the county borders Shropshire, Staffordshire and the great conurbation of Birmingham. To the east is Shakespeare country, Warwickshire; to the south and east Gloucestershire. Westwards the views are into Herefordshire with the Welsh mountains easily picked out from the summits of Bredon and Malvern.

RIVERS AND CANALS

Waterside walking is always a pleasure and there is no shortage of opportunities for round walks or excursions along riverbank or canal towpath with a return by bus or train. The WORCESTER & BIRMINGHAM CANAL (opened 1815) has a hard climb up a watery staircase. From the Severn at Worcester there are some 58 locks to be negotiated in the 30 miles before Birmingham's famous Gas Street Basin is reached. No fewer than 36 form the famous flight at Tardebigge near Bromsgrove, all within 3 miles. The canal builders had other difficulties to overcome: the construction of five tunnels, including the West Hill Tunnel (near Kings Norton), over 2700 yards in length, and Shortwood, 580 yards, north of Tardebigge. Tunnels apart, the towpath is open throughout and a 23 mile stretch between Worcester and Alvechurch is being environmentally improved by British Waterways. There is also a useful cycleway from Perdiswell on the fringe of the city to the centre of Worcester.

Three miles upstream from Worcester Bridge, the DROITWICH CANAL linked the famous salt town with the Severn at Hawford. Derelict for many years restoration is well in hand with the towpath available to walkers. For further information see Chapter 5 and Walk 5b. Access points to the towpath include Hawford (A449) and several small villages located off the A38, Porters Mill, Ladywood, Salwarpe as well as Droitwich.

In 1772 the STAFFORDSHIRE & WORCESTERSHIRE CANAL opened a route from the dedicated canal town of Stourport on the River Severn to the Trent & Mersey Canal and the major arteries of the inland navigation network. Only about 9 of its 46 miles are in the county but it should not be forgotten.

Some 40 miles of Britain's longest river, the Severn, flows through Worcestershire. Once it was the busiest river in Britain with a succession of prosperous river ports. Before the installation of

The Severn in flood and Glovers Needle

locks between Gloucester and Stourport the river, in the most favourable conditions, was navigable beyond Shrewsbury and into Wales as far as Welshpool. The story of the Severn would fill several volumes. Today it is accessible to walkers for most of its length, with paths one or both sides of the river from which many routes can be devised. Remember, however, a there and back outing using both sides of the river needs to take into account that some bridges are set well apart.

Running through the Vale of Evesham is the AVON, Shakespeare's Avon, as some call it. There are several lengths of riverside path available. It was a difficult river for navigation until 1639 when William Sandys financed a series of locks and weirs which opened up the way from Tewkesbury (Glos) to Warwick for ships of up to 30 tons. Access points to the meandering river in

Worcestershire include Eckington Wharf, Pershore's medieval bridge, Evesham and the foot of Cleeve Hill.

The largely untamed River Teme has some riverside ways with the hills above the valley providing further good walking. The river as it neared the Severn south of Worcester achieved a certain fame. At Powick Bridge it had the distinction of providing the power for the first practical large-scale hydroelectric scheme. It was here also that the first shots of the English Civil War were fired in a brief skirmish in September 1642. Nine years later the bridge was partly demolished in the epic battle of Worcester in 1651 when the last shots of those bitter bloody years brought victory to Cromwell and the Parliamentarians.

LONG DISTANCE WALKING

Several long distance paths offer more sustained walking for weekend or longer periods, all of which will be encountered during our explorations. Kinver Edge on the Staffordshire border is the starting point for two of these. The NORTH WORCESTER-SHIRE PATH (26 miles) links several country parks, Kingsford, Clent Hills, Waseley and Lickey Hills (leaflet from the Countryside Service at Waseley Hills Country Park). THE WORCESTERSHIRE WAY (47 miles) makes for the Severn at Upper Arley and after a passage along the river takes to the hills. Whilst completing its journey at the Holly Bush Pass (Malvern Hills) it has link routes to Ledbury and the Severn near Tewkesbury (guide published by Worcester-shire County Council - there is also a free accommodation list).

The WYCHAVON WAY (41 miles) traverses the county from the Severn at Holt Fleet, via Droitwich, the Vale of Evesham, Bredon Hill and on to the Cotswold town of Winchcombe (guide published by Wychavon District Council). The SEVERN WAY shadows the river for most of its length through several counties. (Another of my walking

guides, *Severn Walks* [Cicerone], explores the river and its countryside from its source on Plynlimon to the M48 Severn Bridge that spans the tidal waters.) THE MONARCHS WAY is the most ambitious in concept - a diverse and circuitous 610 miles, it follows the escape route of Charles II after the Battle of Worcester (a guide is published by Meriden Press).

AGRICULTURE AND THE WALKER

The agriculture of an area inevitably affects the quality of the walking available, sometimes enhancing the enjoyment - blossom time in the Vale of Evesham for instance. The footpath network encompasses a wide mix. The wooded hills, towpaths, and the open access areas of commons, country parks and the Malverns present no difficulties. There is a good deal of pasture, both sheep and cattle, not normally a problem for walkers - but remember that grass is a crop and keep to the line of the path. Fruit and vegetables are grown on a large scale particularly in the Vale of Evesham. Cereal crops are more widespread with hop fields prominent around the Teme Valley. Flax (linseed) is becoming slightly more common and there is the inevitable oil seed rape. In these cultivated areas greater care should be taken in way finding with more attention than usual given to the OS map. Lesser used paths may be invisible on the ground but on the basis of "use it or lose it" these have not been ignored in the suggested routes.

PEOPLE AND PLACES

Within this varied countryside people lived and worked, on hilltop forts, stately homes, farms or tied cottages. In the background text to the walks I hope to show a little of their lives and times. Some who, for good or evil, found their way into the pages of history. Others, mostly nameless, who by their skill, artistry or labour helped build the visible monuments, whether it be cathedral or canal, stately home or tithe barn, or shaped the ever changing landscape by forestry, farming or parkland design.

Three great battles that changed or briefly diverted the course of history were fought along the rivers; the Civil War and Worcester have already been mentioned. Just beyond the county boundary a decisive battle in the Wars of the Roses was fought at Tewkesbury in 1471 which secured the throne for the Yorkist Edward IV. While two hundred years earlier, despite the defeat of the Barons and the death of Simon de Montfort at Evesham in 1265, demands for more constitutional government were eventually met.

Before the heavy hand of the Norman conquest was laid upon the land, the Vikings had sailed up the Severn raiding the riverside towns and plundering Worcester Cathedral. In one incident it is said that one of the pillaging party lingered rather too long in an attempt to steal one of the bells. The fury of the populace, recovering from their initial shock, descended upon him and cut off his retreat to the safety of the boat. He was flayed alive and his skin stretched out on the cathedral door. In AD1040 oppressive impositions by the Danes were the cause of much anger in Worcester whose citizens put to death two men sent by the King, Harthacnut, to collect the taxes. His reaction was both swift and violent.

The British Camp on the Malvern Hills is reputed, along with at least half a dozen other sites, to have been the place where Caractacus made his last stand against the Romans. The local tribes do not seem always to have lived at peace with each other, for excavations at the fort on Bredon Hill have revealed evidence of a ferocious attack followed by a massacre before AD100 for which the Romans do not seem to have been responsible.

The walks featured may be followed at any season but it should be remembered that the Severn, Avon and Teme are subject to, sometimes spectacular, flooding. In winter, the Severn, for example, may be 20 feet or more above its summer level. The racecourse at Worcester along with the New Road County Cricket ground is sometimes under water to the depth of 4 feet or more with some of the lower streets providing calmer waters for swans. These conditions will of course be obvious when they have occurred but when the rivers are rising they may do so very quickly. A friend of mine who keeps a boat has noted a rise of 6 feet an hour on occasion.

No time has been quoted for the walks - take them at the pace that suits you - but 2 miles an hour is suggested as an overall benchmark. Most walks take longer than you expect, extended by refreshment breaks, photography, or a leisurely survey of the landscape from some agreeable high point.

The division of this book into the various sections is not faithful to any particular boundary and indeed the areas overlap. There are many places of interest within the county and a general but not exhaustive list is given under Useful Information. Some will be met along the way, but a visit may be appropriate at another time. There are others that seem relevant to include for their diversionary interest.

MAPS AND WAYFINDING

In general, public footpaths and bridleways are signed where they leave the road and many are waymarked - this is especially the case with the long distance routes mentioned above. Yellow arrows denote footpaths, blue arrows bridleways with special logos for regional routes - the Monarchs Way depicts both a ship and Charles II hiding in the famous Boscobel Oak. The Severn Way has a trow - a shallow draught river boat that could be sailed or towed; while the county's famous black pear marks the Worcestershire Way and a pine cone the North Worcestershire Path.

The sketch maps which accompany the route descriptions are not a substitute for the excellent OS maps and their use is strongly recommended. Remember that from time to time footpaths may be diverted or closed for various reasons - timber felling is one. It does not follow that a diversion notice will be in place, the OS map should help you to find a suitable alternative or a legitimate way round an obstruction.

The maps for the areas being explored are listed below - the 1.50000 Landranger series for general use and more usefully for walkers the 1.25000 (2¹/₂ inches to the mile) Pathfinder. These last are in the course of a nationwide revision so before buying check the latest situation. They are being replaced by a new series - Explorer. Covering a much larger area, with greatly improved information, They are superb easy to read maps which are a pleasure to use. There are also additions to the Outdoor Leisure Maps series.

The maps covering Worcestershire (some of which spill over into neighbouring counties) are listed below with the older Pathfinders also quoted at the head of each walk for easy reference.

LANDRANGER 1.50000

138	Kidderminster & Wyre Forest
139 (part)	Birmingham & surrounding area
149 (part)	Hereford, Leominster
150	Worcester, The Malverns and surrounding area

EXPLORER 1.25000

190	(renumbered from Explorer 14) Malvern Hills and Bredon Hill
	for walks 8a, 8b, 8c, 8d, 8e, 8f, 9a, 9b and part 7b
203	Ludlow, Tenbury Wells and Cleobury Mortimer includes part of Worcestershire but no walks on this section
204	Worcester and Droitwich Spa
	for walks 4a, 5a, 5b, 5c, 5d, 6a, 6b, 6c, 7a, 7b (part), 7c (part), 10a, 10b, 10c, 10d
205	Stratford-upon-Avon and Evesham with Alcester
	for walks 4c, 12a, 4d part
218	Kidderminster and the Wyre Forest
	Caution - Note when buying that 218 overlaps on eastern edge with 219
	Walks 2a part only - use 219. 3a, 3c, 3d, 7c part alternative 219
219	Dudley, Wolverhampton and Kidderminster (note western overlap with 218)
	Walks 2a, 2b, 2c and part 2d, 3b, 4b, 7c part - alternative 218
220	Birmingham and Redditch part 2d, 4d (part)

OUTDOOR LEISURE MAP

45	The Cotswolds Walk 11

PREPARATIONS FOR WALKING

(Experienced walkers can skip this section)

No special equipment is required, but boots are strongly recommended. For comfort in all seasons layers of clothing, preferably cotton and wool, are far better than one heavy garment. The selection of waterproof outerwear is important - there is a vast range that is only matched by the wide spread of prices. The industry does well by walkers, climbers and sailors, but it sometimes seems to me that the style image some items provide is in direct ratio to the price charged. Resist the temptation unless you intend some exotic trips and check first to see whether a lighter weight, all year round garment would not be better suited for the conditions generally experienced. A rucksack of about 20 litres capacity will be adequate for day purposes. Look for one with side pockets and quick release fastenings - a bin liner can be pressed into service if the water resistant qualities are in doubt. The contents will of course vary but it should include a first aid kit, a small torch for winter excursions, gloves and head wear according to season - sun can be just as damaging as cold winds. As a hillwalker old habits die hard so my rucksack has a small survival bag as a part of my permanent equipment, and a whistle. Suitable refreshment is of course important, especially liquid - it's a heavy item and for that reason many people don't take enough with them.

It is both wise and rewarding to learn the basic navigation skills of map and compass. Remember to orientate the map to your line of travel - failure to do so may lead to confusion, unintentional trespass, and the embarrassment of having to admit that you are lost.

Finally - dogs, however well behaved, should be kept on a lead where livestock and ground nesting birds are present.

2
The Northern Hills

When Victorian Londoners (and their successors) looked for that much needed breath of fresh air they took the train to Box Hill and the Surrey Downs, or the Thames-side resorts such as Windsor, Maidenhead and Henley. Birmingham people did pretty much the same - their river was the Severn with Stourport, Bewdley and Holt Fleet amongst their destinations. They too headed for the hills: Kinver Edge, for example, where they enjoyed the novelty of tea served from a cave dwelling caterer. The Lickey Hills were a particular favourite bolt-hole with the escape aided by the railway which served the area from the 1840s. These hills might well have gone the way of many another green hill as towns expanded but happily preservation societies and benefactors like the Cadbury family took a hand, and today a large area of the Lickey Hills is owned by the City of Birmingham.

The National Trust acquired part of the Clent Hills, with a country park managed by the Hereford & Worcester County Council, enjoyed by large numbers of people but with ample space for various activities. A descriptive leaflet is available from the Visitor Centre, the Countryside Service or Tourist Information Centres. (The two counties that were united in, for some an unwelcome, marriage in the reforms of 1974 have now divorced and returned to their single status.)

At this point it seems appropriate to relate the ninth century legend associated with the Clent Hills. The story begins not here but at Winchcombe in Gloucestershire, then an important town in the Kingdom of Mercia with a royal palace, mint and an abbey. Aspects of the story are common to all ages: ambition, greed, envy and murder. The addition of certain ornaments, naive belief or perhaps to whip up the pilgrim (tourist) trade to the abbey at Winchcombe, are less common, although not totally absent today.

Reducing a complex story with its conflicting accounts to the bare minimum, it concerns Kenelm who whilst still a boy succeeded to the throne in AD819. His elder sister, Quoenthryth, was resentful to the point that she arranged for the lad to go on a hunting trip to the Clent Hills, where he was murdered. A dove carried a message to Rome which revealed news of the murder and the location of the body - under a thorn tree. The monks of Winchcombe were despatched to investigate. The prince's body was found and taken back to Winchcombe to be enshrined. A holy well gushed forth from the point where he was slain and at other points on the journey back to the Abbey where the body had rested overnight. The young victim is still remembered here - the road through the hills is known as St. Kenelms Pass with the legendary spring head to be seen by the church dedicated to the murdered prince.

Under the northern slopes of the Clent Hills is Hagley Park and the mid-eighteenth century palladian style Hagley Hall, home of the Lyttleton family (open to the public -check times but as a guide Bank Holiday Sundays and Mondays and Sunday to Friday during July and August). The name Lyttleton occurs frequently in the history of the county and the wider world of law, literature, politics and government. One, Alfred Lyttleton, as well as being a distinguished lawyer and politician, had a considerable reputation as an amateur cricketer, keeping wicket for England on a number of occasions. Another member of the family, Sir Charles Lyttelton, was held captive in the Tower of London for his allegiance to Charles I but contrived to escape. Clearly a man of initiative he received various appointments on the restoration of the monarchy. An earlier Lyttleton, John, lost both his fortune and his life for his staunch adherence to his Roman Catholic faith. He was found guilty of high treason following his involvement in the Earl of Essex's rebellion against Elizabeth I. Whilst the sentence was not carried out he died a prisoner in the Tower of London.

2a: Kinver Edge

Starting Point:	Worcestershire County Councils Kingsford Country Park, Kingsford Lane Car Park on west side of Kinver Edge. Grid Ref: 824821.
Distance:	3¼ miles.
Map:	1.50,000 Landranger 138 Kidderminster & Wyre Forest
	1.25,000 Explorer 219 Dudley, Wolverhampton & Kidderminster but note 218 also covers this walk due to overlap (Pathfinder 933 Stourbridge).

NOTES: Woodland walking, with some steep sections followed by fine views from the ridge. A popular weekend outing. If you prefer a quieter time come on a weekday or make a prompt morning start.

Kinver village and most of the Edge which is explored in this walk is in Staffordshire although the 550 feet high ridge continues southwards into Worcestershire and with Blakeshall Common forms part of the Kingsford Country park. At the county boundary, on the ridge above the car park, is the starting point for three regional long distance footpaths: the Staffordshire Way which heads north for some 92 miles to the sham castle on Mow Cop; the

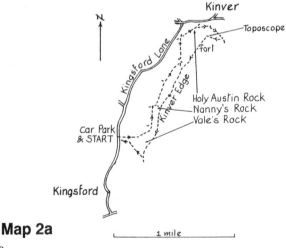

Map 2a

1 mile

Rock dwellings, Holy Austin Rock

Worcestershire Way and North Worcestershire Path, described in the Introduction.

The underlying rock is sandstone, outcropping with spectacular effect and a brilliant orange colour when exposed, friable and soft to work. So much so that a number of rock dwellings were hollowed out, exactly when is uncertain. Not a hair shirt, religious retreat from the world for those opting for the hermit's life of contemplation and study but for ordinary families earning a living on nearby farms and local iron foundries. The area is well wooded, with some oak, conifer plantations and large numbers of silver birch. The man-made caves were an ideal "work from home" opportunity for the besom brush makers of the day. Given the level of home comforts available to most workers of the nineteenth century these houses were not so Spartan as might be supposed. Door and window spaces were excavated, several rooms were available, chimneys were tunnelled upwards through the rock, and some dwellings were on more than one level with the upper storeys commanding an enviable view. Brick frontages improved access at Vale's Rock and a deep well of medieval castle proportions remains.

If all this sounds a long time ago then it should be mentioned that some of the houses were inhabited until the middle of the twentieth century. The sites visited in the walk are Vale's Rock, Nanny's Rock and Holy Austin Rock. The National Trust cares for some 200 acres of Kinver Edge and a few years ago built a house for their warden into Holy Austin Rock and in 1997 completed restoration of the rock dwellings on that site. Wheelchair access has been provided.

Much earlier Iron Age man found a home here with the steep sides of Kinver Edge providing a natural defensive position for a hillfort of about 11 acres, with the usual bank and ditch required on only two aspects.

In the woodland some large parasitic fungi may be seen and the exotic bright red and highly poisonous fly agaric.

THE WALK

Dozens of paths, many not shown on maps, criss-cross the area and may give rise to uncertainty. If you miss the way remember that the outward route heads north-easterly under the Edge to Holy Austin Rock with the much simpler return made along the crest of the ridge.

From the car park cross the road and forward on a broad track into the woodland, with a picnic site and information board to your right. In about 300 yards the towering sandstone outcrop of Vale's Rock, although partly hidden by trees, will be seen facing you. Turn right on a broad track for a few paces then left on a narrow, almost hidden path, in summer camouflaged by Himalayan Balsam, sometimes known as Policemen's Helmet. A few yards of steep ascent will bring you to the first of the rock dwellings, here on two levels.

Retrace your steps down the lower path, turn right and, in a few yards, right again to continue with the gently rising and winding way. After passing a further outcrop of rock on your right reach a small triangular junction, swing right to meet a bridleway in about 100 yards and turn left.

Four hundred yards or so from Vale's Rock the caverns of Nanny's Rock await your inspection. The narrowest of channels cut into the rock gives entrance to the premises, so tight as to provide resistance to a small siege. Here the accommodation is three small rooms and one much larger, with the neighbours just round the corner.

Continue on the undulating path, in 700 yards a sharp climb will bring you to a tiny sandy area and a Y junction of paths. Bear forward left on falling path. In 300 yards at an X junction turn right, signed Holy Austin Rock, and keep ahead (further signs on the way) until you reach a clearing with the road seen ahead. Swing right following posts which direct you to the gated and stepped path to Holy Austin Rock. (Access April - September 9 am to 7 pm, October - March to 4 pm).

Viewing complete, descend on a brick path bearing right towards the woodland and take the middle of three paths. This climbs to a grassy area and at the top turn right, signed to viewpoint. Soon a large clearing lives up to the promise of the sign with a prospect of the roofs of Kinver and the wider world. A toposcope aids the identification of distant points which in the western arc includes Shropshire's Clee Hills, The Long Mynd, and the mysterious Stiperstones. Rather optimistically but perhaps as a comfort to homesick visitors from further afield, London, Edinburgh, Dublin, New York and Moscow are also indicated.

Now head south-west, on the broad track, along the crest of the ridge, taking care not to swing to the left when the ramparts of the hill-fort are met. A triangulation point is passed about 600 yards from the toposcope. In a further half mile the Staffordshire/Worcestershire boundary will be met with picnic site, information board and a signpost for the three regional paths.

Continue for about 300 yards. As you reach a conifer plantation take the descending path on the right. Swing right to the top of Vales Rock to enjoy the adventurous and slightly hazardous viewpoint with its sheer unfenced fall. Here is a fine view over the canopy of the forest, a rare chance to look down upon the birds - it's even better in autumn.

Retrace your steps from Vale's Rock for about 30 yards to turn right and in a few yards at junction of paths bear left soon making a spiral descent to a broad crossing track. Over this, head diagonally right on a falling path to the picnic area and Kingsford Lane.

2b: The Clent Hills

Starting Point:	Nimmings car park, Clent Hills Country Park.
	Hagley Wood Lane, GR 939807. There are further car parks at Walton Hill - GR 943803 and at Adams Hill off Odnall Lane north-west of Clent village
Distance:	5 miles
Map:	1.50,000 Landranger 138 Birmingham
	1.25,000 Explorer 219 Dudley Wolverhampton & Kidderminster (Pathfinder 933 Stourbridge 953 Kidderminster & Bromsgrove).

NOTES: Toilets, refreshments, information, waymarked walks, horseriding and cycle routes.

The CLENT HILLS COUNTRY PARK is larger than most with a network of paths that offer many permutations, increased by making use of routes beyond the park boundaries. This is a walk that proves you don't have to travel great distances from a town to enjoy good country walking in a peaceful atmosphere. Once away from the view to the great Birmingham conurbation you could be almost anywhere in England, such is the variety of the countryside: conifer and broad-leaved woodland, rolling hills with deep valleys, gorse covered heath, sheep pasture, tiny hamlets, little village churches and even a boulder carried here from North Wales by a glacier. The horizons are extensive so pick a clear day, winter or summer to enjoy it to the full - and come again as there is more to see than is included in the route that follows.

THE WALK
From the car park take the stepped path that climbs through trees to the top of the slope and turn right following the inside edge of the wood. Leave by a gate and bear right along the fence following a broad track.

The obelisk seen through the trees is on Wychbury Hill beyond which is an ancient fort. Excavations in the nineteenth century found early Iron Age items.

The track leads to The Four Stones - intriguing yes, but not as ancient as might be thought, being part of the landscaping improvements carried out during the eighteenth century. Other features of that period, not on our route, include a "ruined castle"

24

Map 2b

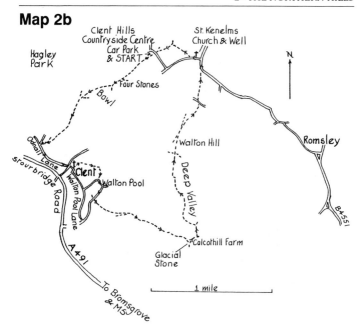

- the romantic folly without which no great park was complete. Capability Brown was one of many hands engaged in the work on the house and extensive grounds of Hagley Hall. Alas the toposcope near The Four Stones is currently without its direction plate.

From the stones (997 feet), go forward, south-west, taking the broad track with the bowl of the "great crater" to your left. This is now followed for half a mile with views that open up to include Hagley Hall. After a while the path descends with Clement Grove seen below to your right.

When a white house is met leave the main track bearing left with the house to your right, soon descending on tarmac - Hill Lane. At the foot turn left on Mount Lane and, in a few yards, left to follow Odnall Lane to the crossroads at St. Leonard's Church, Clent.

(Vine Lane is also known as St. Kenelm's Pass and leads through the hills to the little chapel that bears his name - we shall visit it later in the walk.)

Walking in the Clent Hills

Take the road signed Walton Pool and immediately past the church turn left on a walled and hedged path which leads to the open hillside with more fine views. Head up the slope to the stile to enter the National Trust's Clent Hills property. Go forward but in about 50 yards swing right on a bridleway, continuing beyond a metal gate and descending to the hamlet of Walton Pool.

Turn left with the lane (Walton Rise) and as the houses fall back take the footpath on the left opposite the Foresters Nursing Home. Cross two fields and over a third aiming for the far right corner to turn left on a bridlepath that follows the outside edge of a conifer plantation.

In half a mile Calcothill Farm is approached. Here turn left on a waymarked path, by a boulder carried down from the Arenig Mountain of North Wales in the glacial period. Keep the hedge to your right and in 80 yards turn right to cross a stile with a view down to a deep valley. Turn immediately left from the stile, now on the North Worcestershire Path (pine cone waymarks). Across the valley the thoughtfully landscaped rounded outlines of coniferous woodland climb the slopes with a mix of species to add many shades of green to the hillside. A view that can be enjoyed at leisure with the several seats provided along the way by the Birmingham Wednesday Wanderers Ramblers Club.

After about half a mile the path is signed off forward left. Continue to reach the track by Walton Hill Farm. Cross the track to re-enter the Clent Hills Country Park. Curve right with the bridleway running between gorse to reach the triangulation point on Walton Hill, 1034 feet.

Just short of the triangulation point take the bridlepath forward right. (If you continue past the trig point the track will lead back to the Walton Hill Car Park.) The path descends to meet and turn left on a tarmac lane. Keep left at the road junction and in a few yards take the path on the right. Descend northwards as waymarked to the far corner of the field to meet the road by a private drive. Turn left at the road and shortly left again on Chapel Lane to St. Kenelm's Church where there is a carving of the martyr on the lych gate.

To view the well where legend claims the young prince was murdered in AD820, (see Chapter 2) go through the churchyard turning right to descend steps. An umbrella of ribbons tied to a tree overhangs the spring and as recently as 1985 the spot has been further commemorated by a sculptured water channel.

Retrace your steps and head up the church path from the tower end and in a few yards swing right through the churchyard to cross a small field to a stile. Bear half left to a broken hedgeline and over the next field to turn left on the Penorchard farm track. In about 50 yards turn right, waymarked, and shortly curving left up the steep hillside in the direction of the plantation to meet the road. Here turn right to return to the Nimmings car park, perhaps late in the afternoon to see the pink lit tower blocks of Birmingham.

2c: The Waseley Hills and Chadwich Manor Estate

Starting Point:	Waseley Hills Country Park - north car park.
	Leave M5 at Junction 4, north on the Stourbridge Road A491, then right on B4551 and right at Manchester Inn. GR 971782
Distance::	4³/₄ miles
Map:	1.50,000 Landranger 139 Birmingham

1.25,000 Explorer 219 Dudley Wolverhampton & Kidderminster (Pathfinder 953 Kidderminster & Bromsgrove).

WASELEY HILLS COUNTRY PARK is the HQ of the County Council's Northern Area Countryside Services. A varied programme of guided walks is organised from a number of locations - leaflets are available here and from tourist offices. Facilities include refreshments, information, waymarked routes including the Badger Trail 1¼ miles, Fox Trail 3¼ miles and a running trail.

There are wide ranging views, particularly fine to the west - on a clear day the Welsh mountains over 50 miles distant are readily picked out by those familiar with their profiles. Windmill Hill is 925 feet and Waseley Hill tops the 1000 feet mark. The walk continues to the edge of the Lickey Hills (a City of Birmingham managed park) and through the National Trust's Chadwich Manor Estate. The opportunities for further excursions in the area will become apparent as the suggested walk proceeds.

THE WALK

From the car park head up the hillside, signed Lickey Hills, taking the path to pass the pylon on your right. Looking back there is a wide prospect of the Birmingham area. Make

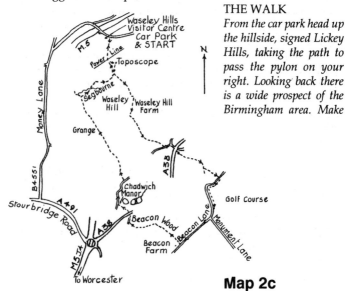

Map 2c

1 mile

for the Windmill Hill toposcope with its all-embracing directional plate which points the way to other fine walking areas within easy reach including the Derbyshire Hillls, the Sugar Loaf near Abergavenny, Hay Bluff, the Clun Forest area of Shropshire, the Long Mynd, the Clee Hills, Black Mixen in the Radnorshire Hills and many more.

From the toposcope go forward for about 250 yards at a slight right diagonal to meet a waymarked post and then on the fenced path, currently the route of the Badger Trail and the Monarchs Way. The path descends on a hollow way with the towers of the closely clustered Birmingham "villages" rearing up on the distant left like some giant legoland.

Maintain your direction - Waseley Hill is to your right - and continue to Waseley Hill Farm (seen on your left) and here cross a stile and bear right on a wide track. In 250 yards or so turn left down the slope, having joined the North Worcestershire Path - pine cone waymarks - to meet a gate and stile. Go forward climbing the hillside with hedge to your left.

In 400 yards bear slight left (NT board near here) to take the falling path to a stile. Continue down the hillside to the southern car park of the Country Park. Turn left with the road, Holywell Lane, and shortly right crossing the A38. Take the bridleway signed just beyond the bridge, a broad rising track at first a hollow way. In just over a quarter of a mile turn left at a metal gate to meet the road in 300 yards.

Cross the road to a tarmac path but bear immediately right to follow the way that runs in parallel with the road i.e. the road is to your right.

We now desert the North Worcestershire Path. Keep to the inside wood edge with many twists and turns for 500 yards until a stile returns you to the road. Turn left - this is Beacon Hill. Cross Monument Lane to continue with Beacon Lane for 500 yards. The Cadbury connection is strong in this area and you will note several name plaques carrying the legend Bournville Village Trust.

Turn right with the bridlepath at Beacon Farm and on via the fenced way through Beacon Wood, which descends steeply. Continue along the inside edge of the wood, to meet a metal gate and on via the tarmac drive of Winsel Cottage to meet a minor road.

SAFETY NOTE. The A38 is just ahead. If this seems to be rather busy you may prefer to turn left using the lane and underpass and rejoin the route beyond Chadwich Manor.

Turn right with the minor road, a dead end, and left to the A38. This is crossed to the opposite bus stop behind which a path heads half left down *to Chadwich Manor - a handsome brick building now past its three hundredth birthday. Continue beyond the buildings to meet a minor road and turn right signed Rubery & Romsley.*

Continue with Redhill Lane, climbing past Spring Pool Cottage to take the path on the left. Bear slight right diagonal to meet a surfaced way and on to join a woodland path signed by a cattle grid. On leaving the wood take a slight diagonal right in the direction of a prominent scots pine, with Chadwich Grange seen to your left.

Beyond a gate go forward on a bridleway lined with beech trees. Keep with this for 500 yards, with gates along the way and passing Segbourne House to your right. When the spring pools are met by Barnes Close bear right on the waymarked permissive path with the stream to your left.

A boardwalk carries you into Segbourne Coppice. Go forward, climbing on a steep and stepped path close to the wood edge. Near the top of the rise ignore a trail signed left and forward 60 yards to a stile and on with the steep bank falling to your left. Curve gently round the top of the deep bowl.

Now turn to look back to the western horizon. The familiar profile of the Malvern Hills is backed by the long line of the Hatterrall Ridge of the Black Mountains ending in Hay Bluff some 50 miles distant. Nearer at hand the Abberley Hills and the Bromyard Downs may be picked out.

Edge along the hedge line and bear right through a break, then left to pass under power line and descend to the Visitor Centre to complete the circuit.

2d: The Lickey Hills

Starting Point:	Lickey Hills Country Park. Visitor Centre is located off the B4096 at the end of Warren Road, GR 998754
Distance:	3, 5³/₄ or 8³/₄ miles
Map:	1.50,000 Landranger 139 Birmingham & surrounding area
	1.25,000 Explorer 219 Dudley Wolverhampton & Kidderminster and Explorer 220 Birmingham & Redditch (Pathfinder 953 Kidderminster & Bromsgrove, 954 Solihull & Alvechurch).

NOTES: All routes include some steep ascents/descents.

This is another good hilly walk using sections of the North Worcestershire Path, the City of Birmingham's Country Park and the towpath of the Worcester & Birmingham Canal. The suggested walk is presented as two connecting loops which meet close to the Visitor Centre. Facilities include refreshments, shop, adventure playground, waymarked walks including a Sculpture and a Wheelchair Trail. The summit of Beacon Hill at the north-west corner of the park is 978 feet. Bilberry Hill close to the centre has a good viewpoint and Cofton Hill peaks at 863 feet. A detailed plan of the park is available at the centre. There is a further car park at the northern end of Monument Lane - GR 985759.

THE WALK

From the car park return towards Warren Road and join the signed bridleway of the North Worcestershire Path (pine cone waymark) found on the right. The way descends to meet and cross the B4096. Go forward on the bridleway but in a few yards bear left through gardens towards the Olde Rose & Crown. Keep ahead passing the inn and cafe to your left, and with a golf course on your right continue into woodland. In a yard or two turn right on a path running along the inside edge of the wood, still with the North Worcestershire Path. In about 200 yards as a crossing path is met bear left and in 20 yards right which shortly curves to the right and in a

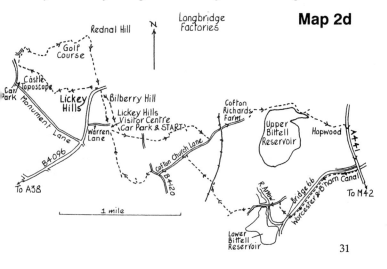

Map 2d

31

further 20 yards turn left to climb a steep and stepped path. This will bring you to the open area of Beacon Hill by a triangulation point. Our route now swings right but a diversion may be in order.

You will have noted an intriguing looking building about 250 yards to the west. This is a fun folly of a castle which houses the toposcope. (It is only a short distance from the Monument Lane car park.) Close by is a commemorative stone which acknowledges the gift in 1907 of Beacon Hill to the City of Birmingham by members of the Cadbury family.

From the triangulation point, cross the open hillside, passing a spring and with the golf course seen below. Continue into woodland and turn right in about 100 yards when a crossing path is met. Descend to meet and turn right with a bridleway - at first on tarmac. (The North Worcestershire Path is abandoned at this point.)

Beyond Rose Cottage continue along the edge of the golf course to join a bridleway under Rednall Hill. Bear right, briefly on tarmac, and continue under trees for half a mile to reach and cross the B4096 to the bridleway used from the Visitor Centre. Take the steep and stepped path forward left to climb Bilberry Hill and on to the fenced viewpoint from which Beacon Hill is prominent in a rolling landscape.

Forward from the viewpoint and when the track divides take the forward right which leads to the upper car park area. Bear right to descend to the Visitor Centre. This completes the first loop.

THE SECOND LOOP

The second and longer loop includes the wider countryside beyond the country park. If continuing from the first loop ignore the division of tracks mentioned above.

If starting anew from the Visitor Centre car park, as you face north take the path on the right and in about 200 yards turn right on a wide stony track. There is a huge contrast, for from the splendid pine forest the view is over the vast acres of Rover's Longbridge factory, sheep pasture and three shimmering reservoirs.

At the end of the car park area join the North Worcestershire Path (pine cone waymarks) which descends on a broad track. After about 200 yards take the stepped path on the left to meet and cross the road. Go forward on a path between houses and over a large field. Pass over a tarmac path and forward to the bottom of the slope where turn right to meet Cofton Church Lane in 350 yards.

The Clent Hills
The Four Stones

Turn left with the lane, continuing with the private road to Cofton Richards Farm. As this is approached cross the stile on the right and immediately left along the hedgerow with the great expanse of Upper Bittell Reservoir away to your right. As the buildings fall back swing right over the field and half left to a stile. Bear right along the hedge and then on a fenced path - the enclosed area to your right is a Site of Special Scientific Interest on the margins of the reservoir.

When the North Worcestershire Path turns sharp left leave it, keep forward to meet a stile and ahead over a field. At the gate/stile go forward on a track to meet the busy A441 at Hopwood. Turn right and in 500 yards right by the Hopwood House Inn to join the towpath of the Worcester & Birmingham Canal. In three-quarters of a mile turn right over bridge 66 following the farm track and path round Bittell Farm to meet and turn left on Bittell Farm Road.

The River Arrow is crossed with Lower Bittell Reservoir to your left. Here in winter a wide variety of ducks may be seen including goosander, smew, golden eye, pochard, widgeon and pintail; osprey have also been spotted.

As the road bends to the left join the field path, heading half left. At a stile turn right to follow the hedge. Note the map shows the hedge to your right and later to your left - waymarking was absent when this was written. At the top of the field bear right to a stile and descend bank and right. In 100 yards the path goes up a stepped bank to cross the railway. *CARE - THIS IS A BUSY MAIN LINE WITH FREQUENT TRAINS.*

Head up the slope with Cofton Hall seen to your right to cross a stile partway down a wire fence and on to the top right corner of the field. Turn left with Cofton Church Lane to reach the main road in a quarter of a mile. Here briefly turn right, signed Rednall, and cross into woodland signed Public Bridleway to Warren Lane - a broad gently rising track. In 300 yards a choice of ways may be made. A stepped path on the right ascends Cofton Hill from which a return may be made to the car park. The view to the trees, which include Douglas Fir, from the lower bridleway is particularly good. If that is your option ignore all left and right turns, continuing to pass a small arboretum to your left. Here is one of the Sculpture Walk exhibits and deserves a closer look. Beautifully carved from a tree trunk it depicts a handsome head - hermaphrodite according to the leaflet, the Spirit of the Woods.

The Visitor Centre is now seen ahead and the walk completed.

3
Kidderminster and the River Ports

Kidderminster lived by the loom, sometimes well, sometimes not. Carpets will no doubt come to mind but the town had been making cloth from the Middle Ages. When Daniel Defoe visited Worcestershire in 1725 he reported that Kidderminster was engaged in the manufacture of linsey woolseys - a rough woollen fabric woven on a cotton warp. It was John Broom who introduced carpet making to the town in the mid-eighteenth century. Cloth making was in one of its periodic declines and Broom, following the example of the Earl of Pembroke who had established carpet weaving at Wilton, travelled to the continent to learn the secrets of the trade. The rest, as they say, is history.

In the centre of the town is a statue which commemorates another local hero, Sir Rowland Hill, 1795-1879. He is best remembered for urging the reform of postal services, being credited with the introduction of the adhesive stamp and the penny post. Fitting therefore that the cost of his statue was raised by a public subscription in stamps. Overlooking the canal and the town is the shining white memorial figure of Richard Baxter (1613-1691) with right hand raised in a benediction. He was chaplain to the Parliamentary Army during the Civil War. Following the restoration of the monarchy he was appointed one of Charles II's chaplains. Often a controversial figure he was forced to quit the Church of England due to the provisions of the Action of Uniformity 1662 but was later able to return to the fold. In 1685 he was tried before the notorious Judge Jeffreys for sedition following publication of *Paraphrase on the New Testament*. Badly treated by the court he was imprisoned until money could be found to pay the substantial fine imposed on one who was clearly a man of conscience deserving of respect rather than the vile abuse heaped upon him by Jeffreys.

Kidderminster is the southern terminus of the Severn Valley Railway which for the most part runs close to the river on its 18 mile journey upstream to Bridgnorth. Intermediate stations and the steam powered trains provide interesting excursions and

34

Rowland Hill the inventor of the penny post, Kidderminster

permutations on the basis of ride out, walk back.

Bewdley earned its living as a port town and from the harvest of the Wyre Forest - timber for boat building, charcoal for furnaces, bark for tanning. Rope making, weaving, brass founding, clay pipes and brewing were counted amongst the towns many industries. For a brief spell it enjoyed a trade in seamen's caps, a type favoured by Dutch sailors and known as Monmouth Caps from the town where they were first made. Todays town is rich in Georgian buildings, has an excellent museum, and a three-arched bridge built to the design of the great civil engineer Thomas Telford. Prince Arthur, who but for his delicate health would have been king instead of Henry VIII, was married (by proxy) at Tickenhill Palace, Bewdley. He and his wife Katherine of Aragon lived here for a brief time. The towns most famous connection of more recent years is the three times prime minister Stanley Baldwin, 1867-1947. He held that office during the General Strike of 1926 and later during the difficult period surrounding the abdication of Edward VIII in 1937. For a detailed history of the town readers are referred to *Bewdley in its Golden Age* compiled by the Bewdley Historical Research Group.

A walk which includes the Wyre Forest follows this chapter but other forest walks may be started from Bewdley itself, Callow Hill

(A456) where there is a small visitor centre and from car parks off the B4194 north-west of the town. A walk downstream on the east bank of the Severn will bring you to Blackstone Rock. A cave here was once home to a learned recluse and during the Second World War was pressed into service as a hopefully bombproof depository for the precious dies of a local porcelain factory.

Stourport-on-Severn was the product of the canal age, built to service the traffic between the Severn and the Staffordshire & Worcestershire Canal. A continuous path follows the east bank of the Severn to Holt Fleet - 6 miles. A walk of about a mile downstream on the western bank of the river will bring you to the Redstone Rock Hermitage with extensive "accommodation" in the hollowed out caves reputed to date back to the twelfth century. Close to Stourport is Hartlebury Common, which provides pleasant strolling over sandy heath country. Nearby is Hartlebury Castle, traditionally the seat of the Bishops of Worcester with a fine banqueting hall and an excellent folk and carriage museum.

3a: Heart of Oak - The Wyre Forest

Starting Point:	Upper Arley, signed off the A442, 4 miles north of Kidderminster. For car park turn right on a narrow lane when you reach the River Severn.
Distance:	7¹/₂ miles
Map:	1.50,000 Landranger 138 Kidderminster & Wyre Forest
	1.25,000 Explorer 218 Kidderminster & The Wyre Forest (Pathfinder 952 Wyre Forest & Cleobury Mortimer tiny portion of 932 Highley)

The WYRE FOREST is "one of Britain's largest surviving native oak woodlands." These are the words that welcome visitors to English Nature's reserve in part of the once extensive forest. The suggested circuit explores easy to follow paths and rides with a return along the banks of the Severn. Look for kingfisher and heron along the Severn and the forest streams. If lucky you may catch a glimpse of fallow deer. Fox, badger and adder are also to be found in the forest and feral mink have been seen along the Dowles Brook. The sound of a day hunting owl may be heard at any time of the year and in spring as the new leaf appears the woods are rich in birdsong.

UPPER ARLEY is a small Severn-side village with its sandstone church standing high above the river. In spring snowdrops line the path to the church. In the chancel there is a monument to Sir Walter de Balun. The manner of his death in AD1270 would not be out of place in a medieval costume drama (*Ivanhoe* comes to mind!). The knight had elected to join Prince Edward, the future Edward I, on what was to be the last crusade to the Holy Land. Sir Walter was to marry a daughter of Ralph Mortimer, the Earl of March. The wedding took place while the expedition waited to board ship at Southampton. On the day of the marriage a tournament had been arranged, and Sir Walter was scheduled to join the jousting. Why a man who had just been wed is getting involved in such dangerous sports is a mystery. No doubt his mind was not totally engaged on the contest for he was badly injured and died of his wounds. His widow had the body brought back to Arley for burial.

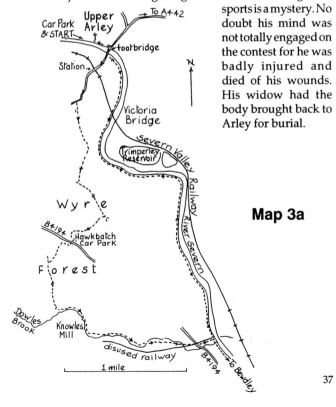

Map 3a

Another tragedy is recorded on the memorial to the Hon. Henry Annesley, son of the Earl of Mountnorris"...the circumstances attending his death were most affecting and awful. When bathing in the sea at Blackpool he was borne away by the violence of the waves...".

The crossing of the Severn along most of its length was often a problem. Bridges were few and far between and apt to be swept away in the swollen waters of winter. Ferries were numerous, although I believe only two still operate today. One such crossing with heavy traffic was at Upper Arley. The Victoria County History records the existence of a ferry here which was a source of profit to the Lord of the Manor in the fourteenth century. He also enjoyed the benefits accruing from a fish weir which seems to have been in place in 1236 and probably a good deal earlier, and a corn mill. The building of the Severn Valley Railway Station beyond the western bank no doubt contributed to the income from the ferry's operation for a time. The chain operated ferry closed in the 1960s and was eventually replaced by a pedestrians only box bridge.

THE WALK

From the car park retrace your steps to follow the road to just beyond the village stores. Turn right over the footbridge which provides such a good view of Upper Arley in its river setting. Take the rising lane passing the Harbour Inn and over the railway bridge.

If Arley station looks familiar then you may have seen the BBC television comedy *Oh Doctor Beeching*. This does duty as the rather over-staffed "Hatley". The threat of closure hanging over the little country station was just as real as this very British comedy depicts. If the humour was not sophisticated it was always worth watching for the nostalgia of the railway, with the engine puffing round a curve in the line or disappearing under a bridge.

Remain with the lane for a further 500 yards and at a bend take the signed path on the left, immediately passing a pond and disregarding a path to the right. The good track rises to the woods, giving views over the Severn valley and to the blue circle of Trimperley Reservoir, at weekends dotted with small sailing boats.

Just beyond the gateway at the wood edge leave the track and forward half right on a climbing path. As you reach the end of an open area ignore the right turn but in a few yards bear right to follow the path that runs above a deep valley with a steep bank broken by rocky outcrops to your right.

At a large fallen tree with branches spread like a giant spider the track bears slight left (keep the valley to your left if the tree has gone). As the cleft narrows to a springhead turn left on a wide track, soon to meet a junction of paths. Go forward on a broad forest track.

In 400 yards a brick structure is passed (on your left) marked "location 125", apparently an underground reservoir perhaps for fire-fighting. In 250 yards take the path on the right and after 300 yards cross a wider track. The path curves to the right as a car park is seen through the trees. In 200 yards bear left at a junction to meet a metalled road at the Hawkbatch car park by a Forest Enterprise information board.

Turn right on the approach road soon to meet and cross the busy B4194 and bear right on the broad track along the inside edge of the wood. In about 200 yards turn left on a wide track to meet a junction of paths in 400 yards. Bear left heading directly south as indicated by an old sign which reads "Coopers Mill Youth Centre and Dowles Brook".

Ignore the first turn to the right and 200 yards on, as the track curves right, go forward on a lesser, grassy, descending path. Keep forward as a track comes in from the right and continue until an English Nature information board is met near the foot of the hill. Here turn sharp left to follow the valley of the Dowles Brook downstream.

Once the fast flowing stream powered several mills. Upstream is Coopers Mill, our way passes the attractive grey stone buildings of Knowles Mill, and further on Town Mill is seen.

At first the stream is to your right, with rocks outcropping from the steeply banked and wooded slopes to the left. Beyond the mills a further house is passed and the Dowles Brook crossed. Leave the track as it curves right to meet a minor road, bearing left through the Fred Dale Nature Reserve. Continue with the often muddy track passing Dowles Manor beyond the brook and hemmed in by the high embankment of a disused branch line on your right.

On reaching the road turn right. Beyond the bridge abutments take the footpath on the left which follows the brook to meet the Severn. Turn left, passing the high pillars securely anchored to the bed of the river but now relieved of the burden of carrying a branch line of the Severn Valley Railway over the volatile waters.

From hereon the way is easy to follow with waymarked stiles leading *to field paths and woodland ways alongside the Severn for the next 2 ¾miles. This part of the river is some miles beyond today's limit of the Severn navigation but canoeists and "rafters" may be seen - occasionally even a coracle, the oldest craft on the river.*

The Severn Valley Railway shadows the opposite bank but crosses the river by the Victoria Bridge of 1861, an iron structure cast and erected by the famous Coalbrookdale Company. If Arley station was not familiar then this bridge may induce a sense of déjà vu for it has appeared in films and TV many times.

Upper Arley is announced by the houses rising from the riverside and its handsome church set on the ridge. Cross the footbridge and turn left to return to your starting point.

3b: The Stour Valley - Cookley and Wolverley

Starting Point:	Kingsford Country Park, Blakeshall Lane car park on eastern side of Kinver Edge on minor road about 1 mile south-west of Kinver village, GR 836821
Distance:	7 miles
Map:	1.50,000 Landranger 138 Kidderminster & Wyre Forest
	1.25,000 Explorer 219 Dudley Wolverhampton & Kidderminster but note that the 218 overlap covers part. (Pathfinder 933 Stourbridge, 953 Kidderminster & Bromsgrove).

NOTES: The County Council have plans to install a picnic site at Caunsall nearer to the canal.

This walk follows the North Worcestershire Path (pine cone waymarks) and then joins the towpath of the Staffordshire and Worcestershire Canal as it makes its way through the Stour Valley towards Kidderminster. It seems that the Stour (or its glacial forebear) was once much wider for both sides of the valley rise steeply, so much so that in places it is bounded by sandstone cliffs. The river meanders about the valley bottom in apparently aimless fashion. The terrain has similarly dictated that the canal runs rather less straight than most, with several appreciable curves that greatly improve its aesthetic appearance over the straight cut that its engineers and financiers would have doubtless preferred.

Feral mink are found in the area and a British Waterways worker told me of finding them comfortably ensconced in the cabin of his workboat. Commercial traffic no longer uses the canal which links the Severn at Stourport with the Trent and Mersey near Stafford. It was therefore a surprise to find, one winter's day, a narrowboat carrying coal for sale to canalside premises.

THE WALK

From the car park turn right with Blakeshall Lane (or initially follow the parallel path just inside the wood). In 500 yards join the signed North Worcestershire Path, found on the left just after passing a pond. In 150 yards bear left to make a long easy descent (³/₄ mile) through gently rolling landscape and passing the well appointed livery stables at Slad Barn.

Map 3b

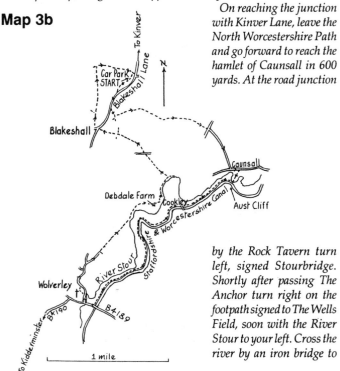

On reaching the junction with Kinver Lane, leave the North Worcestershire Path and go forward to reach the hamlet of Caunsall in 600 yards. At the road junction

by the Rock Tavern turn left, signed Stourbridge. Shortly after passing The Anchor turn right on the footpath signed to The Wells Field, soon with the River Stour to your left. Cross the river by an iron bridge to

41

join the canal towpath as you face the 30 feet high Aust Cliff. Turn right, to follow the canal for nearly 2 miles. This is an attractive passage with the still waters reflecting darkly ancient oaks, the muted colours of moored narrowboats or more brightly, white painted cottages. The Cookley tunnel is reached in half a mile, a modest affair compared to many, only about 193 feet long.

You emerge from the darkness of the tunnel to the sound of industry - a foundry - following an established tradition for a forge was operating here before 1800.

Debdale Lock is met in 300 yards beyond which the way is through wooded countryside with a succession of sandstone cliffs. Continue beyond Forge Bridge to reach Wolverley Lock and the eponymous pub. It carries an inscription across the bulwarks of a model narrowboat: "Life in the slow lane unspoilt by progress".

Turn right with the main road, now with Wolverley church prominent on its sandstone bluff. Turn right again signed Kingsford Country Park. Soon take the path on the left which climbs to the church. (It may be locked but there is a good view.) Descend by the stepped path cut through the sandstone, a slightly eerie atmosphere on a dark day.

WOLVERLEY is worlds away from the bustle of nearby Kidderminster. If you have entered the village by the road rather than the church steps you will have noticed the cottages partly built in the living rock. Bear left to the car park behind the Queens Head. Here rock dwellings and store places have been cut deep into the cliff upon which the church stands.

John Noakes, the Worcestershire historian, recounts a legend connected with the village. Sir John Attwood of Wolverley Court departed on one of the many crusades to the Holy Land and being captured languished long in the Saracens dungeons. In due time his wife assumed his death and was about to marry when a miracle occurred. Sir John in his anguish prayed that if he could only be released he would give much of his fortune to the work of the church. Amazingly he awoke from a deep sleep to find himself lying in a field in his home village still wearing his prison chains. He was, so it is said, reunited with his more than surprised wife just in time to prevent her remarriage.

Continue with the village road with a fine group of buildings on your right: Court House, the Old School House, Knights House of 1829 etc.

These were part of Sebright School, founded as the date on Court House suggests in 1620 under the will of Sir William Sebright. Sir William died without issue and used his fortune in many charitable works, putting the church into good order, repairing the Stour bridges. Such was his beneficence that he became known as the "father of the poor".

Keep with the road, cut through sandstone, which continues beyond traffic lights, passing the Live and Let Live. About 80 yards after Drakelow Lane on your left, turn right on The Short Yard, which beyond a gate continues as a broad track. As the farm track swings right, keep ahead now on a grassy way. Continue, now climbing through Gloucester Coppice with the Stour and the canal seen below.

Back in the open, go forward with a hedge to your right. As this falls back cross the field descending a steep slope and on through a gateway into the Debdale Farm complex. Keep metal barns to your left and bear right then left along the broad drive with the Stour on your right. In about 300 yards turn sharp left up the steep wooded slope. From a stile go forward with the boundary to your left. Thence over next field to meet a lane and turn left for a few yards before joining the hedged bridleway on your right.

The bridleway is now followed for 700 yards to meet Blakeshall Lane. Take the path opposite which curves to follow a wide track and on into woodland. Go through the gate marked Horses but in a few yards join the path on the left, but forward, ie. heading northwards. Maintain your direction under the shelter of scots pine and other conifers for 600 yards. At the fourth intersection turn right soon passing Kinver Edge Farm and open fields to your left to return to your starting point.

3c: Jacobs Ladder and Habberley Valley

Starting Point:	Trimpley - Bus stop/telephone box, GR 791785 or Habberley Valley Car Park - see notes.
Distance:	4^{1}/$_{4}$ miles
Map:	1.50,000 Landranger 138 Kidderminster & Wyre Forest
	1.25,000 Explorer 218 Kidderminster & Wyre Forest (Pathfinder 952 Wyre Forest & Cleobury Mortimer 953 Kidderminster & Bromsgrove).

NOTES: There is no formal parking at Trimpley but the walk has been described from that point since a bus service, 297, operates between Kidderminster & Bridgnorth - two hourly, not Sundays or evenings - see

Useful Information for contact number. (There is a small lay-by about 500 yards from the Trimpley start point - this is found beyond Trimpley church.) Motorists may prefer to start from the Habberley Valley car park reached from the B4190. There is a small county council visitor centre and waymarked walks. A shorter excursion may be enjoyed strolling round this wooded valley.

The suggested route explores hilly country through woodland, deep valleys, open fields with many good views and some steep ascents balanced by periods of level walking.

THE WALK

From the bus stop/telephone box head back along the lane in the direction of Kidderminster ie., south-east. Ignore the first path signed left but just after passing Trimpley Farm take the path on the left which follows the inside woodland edge to reach a lane by The Mount in a quarter of a mile.

Turn left and in 250 yards take the signed path on the right to make the long stepped descent via Jacob's Ladder. At the foot of the ladder there is a confusion of paths. Go forward, then as paths divide keep ahead leaving the marker post 9Z on your right. When the path divides again keep ahead, with a sheer cliff seen to your left, to reach the bottom of the Habberley Valley. Here turn right to follow the valley through broadleaved woodland soon passing the huge sandstone outcrop of Pekket Rock. After passing the Visitor Centre keep forward - Yew Tree House away to the right has a realistic figure of a deer at its gate. Keep with the main track southwards and on beyond the car park sign.

If following the route from Habberley Valley car park retrace your steps down the track.

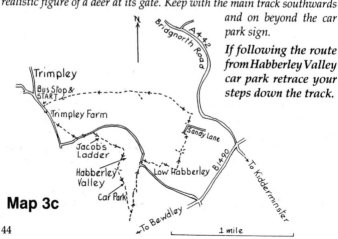

Map 3c

44

In about 300 yards, as a clump of pines is seen on the right, fishhook left on a path that climbs the hillside. Ignore the first right turn but about 150 yards after leaving the main track curve right up the hillside. At the top of the hill bear left on a bridleway on the inside edge of the wood which continues as a hedged path between fields to reach Low Habberley.

Go forward with the road, Valley Close, crossing the Kidderminster Road to the Trimpley Road. In 100 yards take the signed path on the right. As a metal gate is reached turn left through a gap in the hedge and immediately right. (The paths have been re-routed in this area so may not match some maps.) Follow the clear path along the variable geometry of the field edge. After about 400 yards the hedge swings sharp right - leave it to turn directly left to a powerline pole.

Continue with the hedge to your left until the track from Low Habberley Farm is met. Turn left with this for a few yards then resume your direction for 300 yards. Turn left on a footpath with the hedge to your left shortly to cross a waymarked stile and immediately right on Sandy Lane.

Keep with the lane as it swings right but in a few yards take the path on the left which crosses two fields to the valley bottom. Cross a small stream by a plank bridge and turn left up the narrow valley guarded by sandstone cliffs. In 400 yards recross the stream and turn right to a stile. Ignore the path signed off left - beyond a further stile your fenced path gradually climbs high above the stream.

After emerging into the open go ahead on a grassy farm track to a gate. Here go forward on the track that leads to Easthams Farm but after a short distance join the path waymarked on the left, curving right with it to follow the stream. At the next stile head up the steep hillside to a gate almost opposite but reached by an elliptical path which eases the steepest part of the ascent. From here there are good views to Kidderminster and the wider landscape.

Cross the next rising field to the stile set partway along the opposite boundary (about the seventh tree in from the left but I note some felling is taking place). From here forward cross roughly between two trees towards the top left of the field.

At a gate/stile turn left along the hedgerow, over a stile and plank bridge to reach the road by Bite Farm. If you started from Trimpley turn right towards the bus stop to complete the circuit. If you joined the route at Habberley Valley turn left to pick up the path beyond Trimpley Farm and follow route instructions to Jacob's Ladder etc.

3d: Eymore Wood and the Severn

Starting Point: Eymore Wood car park, Trimpley, GR 776793 or Severn
Trent picnic site about 150 yards westwards.

Distance: 3¹/₂ miles

Map: 1.50,000 Landranger 138 Kidderminster & Wyre Forest.

1.25,000 Explorer 218 Kidderminster & Wyre Forest
(Pathfinder 952 Wyre Forest & Cleobury Mortimer.932
Highley)

NOTES: Eymore Wood is a private wood with waymarked walks including
access to the Worcestershire Way. The Severn Trent picnic site also gives
access to woodland and the River Severn via paths round parts of the
Trimpley Reservoir.

Pine forest, oak woodland, open landscape and riverbank are part
of the menu for this walk, completed by a touch of the seaside with
white sails bobbing on the blue waters of the Trimpley Reservoir.
Watch for deer, tree creepers and jays. This is a boots walk in winter
or after heavy rain.

THE WALK·
*From the car park walk down the lane to the end of the public road by the
entrance to the Severn Trent premises (no admittance). Take the bridleway*

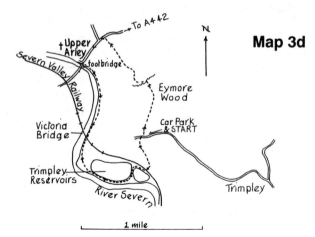

on the right and keep to the broad track through coniferous woodland. In 200 yards the Worcestershire Way is crossed. Continue ignoring all left and right turns. After passing a corrugated iron building on your left the track descends to cross a stream. Bear left with this but soon rising to leave the wood and curving right on a broad, fenced track.

After 200 yards the way may appear to divide. Curve left with a hedge to your right and the tower of Arley church glimpsed in the distance. A further quarter of a mile will bring you to a lane. Turn left to descend to Upper Arley village - about 400 yards. (Upper Arley is described in Walk 3a.)

There is soon a view over the river to the Severn Valley Railway station. The footbridge which replaced an ancient ferry is met as the road turns right. Descend steps. Do not cross the bridge but keep left to follow the Severn downstream, a route shared by the Worcestershire and Severn Ways. This is a rising and falling path, in places a good 40 feet above flood levels, later apt to be inundated, although slightly higher paths are available.

In 500 yards the Worcestershire Way departs after the path falls to cross a small bridge. The Severn Way and our route continue with the riverside under trees with a steep cliff lying back a little, no doubt a relic from when the Severn was wider - perhaps from the time when a great lake which had formed further north burst its banks to allow the river to sweep southwards, creating the Ironbridge Gorge and revealing some of the area's mineral wealth as it cut its way through.

Three-quarters of a mile downstream from Upper Arley pass under the fine single span Victoria Bridge, cast in iron in 1861 for the Severn Valley Railway, at Coalbrookdale, home of the Industrial Revolution. In 200 yards the path emerges into the open with the green banks of the Trimpley Reservoir making an amphitheatre-like curve echoed by the dark wooded cliffs on the western side of the river.

In a short distance climb the stepped and signed path to the top of the reservoir bank and bear right along the water's edge. Continue beyond the bridge with a further reservoir to your right. In 100 yards descend by steps to cross a tarmac road and go forward, signed Eymore Wood Car Park, between the railway and the second reservoir.

After 200 yards or so bear left to cross the railway track into woodland and continue on a rising path. This soon divides. Take the left forward fork which after climbing steeply decants onto the lane. Turn right to return to your starting point.

4

Bromsgrove and Redditch

REDDITCH is a new town built round an old town. Many industries thrive here now but once its economy was balanced on a fine point - that of a needle. The invention of the needle must come a close second to the wheel as being of greatest benefit to mankind. The history of this everyday item is celebrated in the unique Forge Mill Museum, Redditch.

By the mid-sixteenth century needle-making had flourished in London for some time but during the next hundred years dissatisfaction with the regulations being enforced by the Livery Company the manufacture spread beyond the capital to a number of other towns. The Great Fire of London in 1666 contributed to the further dispersal with moves which included relocation to Long Crendon in Buckinghamshire. But the needle makers were soon on the move again and the covered wagons rolled into Astwood Bank to bring the needle industry to the Redditch area.

The Forge Mill Museum concentrates on needle manufacture from 1730, the year when the mill was converted to carry out the scouring or polishing that completed the manufacturing process, although needles had already been in production in the area for at least a century before. The range of the needle is most widely demonstrated in a glass case that contains "Eve's needle" of 7000 years ago and a surgical needle that "ensured the successful flight of the most technologically advanced vehicle ever built...", a reference to the space shuttle for which a Redditch-made needle was used "to hand sew the silica cloth thermal barriers in orbital thermal protection systems". From needles to fish hooks is a small leap, thence to fly tying and rod making, all carried on at Redditch and exported across the world.

Close to the Forge Mill is the Bordesley Abbey Visitor Centre. Excavations continue to reveal more of this major Cistercian foundation.

BROMSGROVE too is an old town but may be best known for its association with the poet and latin scholar, A. E. Housman of *A*

Shropshire Lad fame whose statue is to be found in the High Street. A leaflet describing the signed Housman Trail, a $1^{1/4}$ mile walk or 6 mile motor route, is available from the Tourist Information Centre.

The parish church, St. John the Baptist, is well worth a visit, open Saturdays 11am to 3.30pm, or key from the vicarage. In the churchyard side by side are the gravestones of two martyrs of the railway age, engine drivers Thomas Scaife and Joseph Rutherford. Both were killed in 1840 when the boiler of their ironically named engine "Surprise" burst. The story of the tragic accident is told on the gravestones. A verse typical of the time inscribed for Thomas Scaife begins:

> "My engine now is cold and still,
> No water does my boiler fill,
> My coke affords its flame no more,
> My days of usefulness are o'er
> My wheels deny their wonted speed
> No more my guiding hands they heed
> My whistle too has lost its tune"

Later lines include:

> "No more I feel each urging breath
> My steam is now condensed in death
> Life's railway o'er each station past"

In Birmingham Road just beyond the High Street there is a small well ordered local museum. The cottage industries of the past feature strongly. Nail-making was one, with the entire family engaged in the work usually operating from a garden shed. It was hard work and most families were desperately poor. Glass making was another small family business which expanded through intermarriage.

The Lickey Incline with its testing gradient on the eastern side of Bromsgrove is part of railway history. The 2 mile long pull up towards Birmingham required a pair of extra engines to help trains on their way, pushing from behind. Later a specially built and famous locomotive, affectionately known as Big Bertha, performed this operation for many years and is represented in the museum by its whistle.

The Bromsgrove Guild of Craftsmen, which was founded by a local schoolmaster in 1894, is also featured. One of its functions was to aid the marketing of the many skills of the town which included cabinet-making, metalwork, decorative plaster and stained glass. In 1904 a commission was received to make the gates for Buckingham Palace. Another prominent public work was the famous Liver birds of Liverpool. A street of suitably stocked shops of the Victorian/Edwardian era has its own fascination. The photographer's array of ancient equipment includes an enormous bellows camera which belonged to Herbert Austin the motor manufacturer.

*The Old Engine House, Worcester & Birmingham Canal
at Tardebigge flight*

4a: The Tardebigge Flight

Starting Point: Picnic Site by Tardebigge church. Located off the minor road which runs parallel with the A448 between Bromsgrove & Redditch, GR 996692

Distance: 5 miles

Map: 1.50,000 Landranger 139 Birmingham and small section of Landranger 150 Worcester, The Malverns

1.25,000 Explorer 204 Worcester & Droitwich Spa (Pathfinder 974 Droitwich)

NOTES: Mainly level walking

Tardebigge church, St. Bartholomew's is distinctive by any standards with a tower topped by a fine pointed spire with lancet openings and further embellished with four great urns. A landmark since it was built in 1777, it occupies the high ground above the rising valley which the canal builders chose as the most practical route for the Worcester & Birmingham Canal. What the other options might have been civil engineers may shudder to think.

This walk follows the canal down the watery staircase provided by the longest flight of locks in the British waterways system. Of the 58 locks between the Severn and Birmingham, 30 of these are in the Tardebigge flight in a stretch that is a little under 2 miles, with a further 6 locks within the next mile to Stoke Prior.

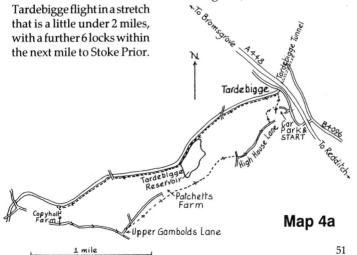

Map 4a

THE WALK

From the car park take the path that curves downhill to join the towpath. To your right is the entrance to the 580 yard long Tardebigge Tunnel but our route swings left to follow the canal for 2 miles. (Not quite the full length of the lock flight.)

Opposite is the cluster of buildings which serve as the canal maintenance depot, moorings, car parking and the start of a short circular waymarked walk. You may also see the narrowboat operated by the Dudley Canal Trust which offers tunnel trips (Tel. 01384 232275). All combine on a still day to provide a delightful mirror image in the water which belies their inherently utilitarian purpose.

Lock number 58, Tardebigge Top Lock, marks the start of the long descent. The canal is broad but the locks are narrow and deep. Overlooking lock 57 and with a fine view is the former engine house/pumping station that kept the system supplied with water drawn from the Tardebigge Reservoir. This is now a restaurant, Tylers Lock on the Water (Banks Brewery).

Soon you are sandwiched between the glasslike waters of the reservoir and the canal. At lock 53 the date on the lock-keeper's cottage is 1791. During the winter of 1997/98 extensive repair work to crumbling brick and stone work was in progress. The drained section of the waterway afforded a picture of the canal in skeleton much as the navvies would have seen it as they completed their work.

A few yards before the first gate of lock 33 is reached (it is the one with the swing footbridge) we leave the canal, taking an almost hidden path on the left that falls down the canalbank to a stile. Cross a narrow field, slight left, and over a footbridge. Continue along the hedge of a rising field to reach the road by Copyholt Farm and turn left with Copyholt Lane for half a mile.

Turn left on Upper Gambolds Lane and in 200 yards take the bridleway on the right. (Care - NOT the footpath signed immediately before.) Should the bridleway prove excessively churned up continue with the lane for a further 300 yards and turn right on a surfaced footpath which will link with our route.

At first the bridleway is hedged but beyond a wooden gate emerges into a field. Go forward soon to bear right with a surfaced track which leads to Patchetts Farm in 600 yards. Continue keeping the farm buildings to your left, then follow the field edge. The gently rising ground provides views with the reflective waters of the reservoir below, the old engine house and more distantly Bromsgrove church.

Ponds, wet and dry, are passed to left and right and in a little over half a mile from the farm a road junction is met. Go forward on High House Lane, soon passing farm and houses. Six hundred yards after joining the lane take the signed path on the left (briefly joining the Monarchs Way) which crosses playing fields to reach the churchyard, and turn right to return to your starting point.

4b: Chaddesley Woods

Starting Point:	The church, Chaddesley Corbett
Distance:	5¹/₂ miles
Map:	1.50,000 Landranger 139 Birmingham and surrounding area.
	1.25,000 Explorer 219 Dudley, Wolverhampton & Kidderminster. (Pathfinder 953 Kidderminster & Bromsgrove).

NOTES: Woodland and field paths - mainly gentle slopes.

CHADDESLEY CORBETT is a place of tranquillity midway between the clamour of Kidderminster and the bustle of Bromsgrove. Long settled - it was listed in the Domesday Book of 1086 by William the Conqueror's tax assessors - it is one of Worcestershire's almost hidden treasures without artificiality or commercialism. Along the village street tall brick Georgian houses are set close to older timber framed buildings in happy haphazard fashion.

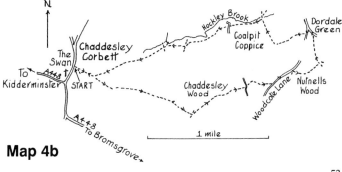

Map 4b

The church too is distinctive, reflecting many centuries and is, unusually, dedicated to St. Cassian. If this is the early Christian martyr who was a schoolmaster then it is in part appropriate for close by is the school rebuilt and enlarged by James Pratt in 1809. Unhappily the church's patron saint met a violent end - stabbed to death by the pens of his pupils. The village treated its teachers more kindly - a house bears a plaque which reads "This house was built in the year 1785 for the use of the schoolmaster of the parish and the sum of sixty pounds given by the late Mr. Clement Fisher was expended thereon".

Chaddesley Woods too are special - an English Nature reserve and to quote from the information board "... a fragment of the great royal hunting forest of Feckenham". It is an attractive mix of broadleaved - mostly oak - and coniferous trees. As the firs mature they will be felled and this ancient natural woodland allowed to regenerate itself. Woodpeckers will be heard if not seen and watch for deer slots in the mud - muntjac have been mentioned. These are the size of a large dog with a not dissimilar bark. Escaping from collections in the nineteenth century they have prospered in the wild, notably the Chilterns. Several rights of way run through the woods but other paths are "out of bounds" to the public except for white arrowed paths that are part of the Jubilee Walk.

THE WALK
From the church head up the village street and opposite The Swan take the path signed Chaddesley Wood, passing the long timber framed building of the Old Malt House. Soon the path divides at a Y junction. Take the left and go forward to a stile. Continue on a wide track passing Vicarage Farm on your left. When the track veers right, keep ahead at first with the hedgerow to your left, and over fields and under a power line to enter Chaddesley Wood - just under a mile from the village. As you climb to the wood turn to look back over a gentle green landscape backed by distant hills. Titterstone Clee is seen to the left of the church and Brown Clee, at 1772 feet the highest point in Shropshire, to the right. Both carry monuments of modern communications technology, the first a satellite navigation "golf ball" while masts reach skywards from the second.

Take the forward path from the woodland stile. As a wider track is met bear right soon climbing to meet a T junction of broad tracks - well waymarked from here. Bear left and continue under pines ignoring all left and right turns to reach a further information board in about 500 yards. Cross a stile and swing left along the outside edge of the wood to meet and cross a lane in a quarter of a mile.

Go forward on the inside edge of Santery Hill Wood for 300 yards and continue on a tarmac drive to meet and turn left on Woodcote Lane. In 300 yards take the footpath on the right, NOT the bridleway. Cross a short field to enter Nutnells Wood following a narrow path to reach a stile at the wood edge in just over 200 yards. Follow the field margin with the wood to your left and at the bottom go over a stile and turn back into woodland. Cross two plank "bridges" to follow a narrow winding path northwards for 400 yards. Leave the wood to cross a small field to reach Dordale Road by a white farmhouse.

Turn left with the road and left again at a junction, Woodcote Lane. In 50 yards take the footpath on the right and ahead to meet a stile and carry on with a ditch and an old orchard to your left. At the foot of the field turn right with Coalpit Coppice to your left, later passing a pool. At the end of the field go forward under trees to a stile and footbridge by Hockley Brook. Cross the stile but not the bridge and bear left on a narrow path to meet and cross a second bridge. Bear right to a stile and forward over fields to meet the road in 500 yards.

Turn left and in a few steps join a path on the right to a stile at the far left corner of the field. Go forward through a scrubby area soon curving left up a bank to emerge into the open. Bear right with a hedge to your right at first and continuing up a slope to a gap in the hedgerow. Bear half right to a stile under a pylon.

The hitherto excellent waymarking is now briefly interrupted, presumably because it is not physically possible to follow the right of way as shown on the definitive map published as far back as 1989. The nearest approximation is therefore detailed below.

From the stile cross a field and over a farm drive, and on to an exit near the far left corner of the field. Now go straight ahead crossing three fields with Hockley Brook to your right. Cross a hedged track and on to a stile halfway down the next boundary. Here bear slight right over a large field to a break in the hedge with the church seen ahead. Cross an even larger field in the direction of a farmhouse to meet a track and turn right to retrace your steps to the village via the allotments.

4c: *Abbots Morton and Inkberrow*

Starting Point:	Abbots Morton church.
Distance:	5¹/₂ miles
Map:	1.50,000 Landranger 150 Worcester & The Malverns
	1.25,000 Explorer 205 Stratford-upon-Avon & Evesham
	(Pathfinder 997 Stratford-upon-Avon - West)

NOTES: No great drama in the landscape - just pleasant field paths with mainly gentle slopes.

ABBOTS MORTON is a small, well kept, black and white village 8 miles south of Redditch and close to the Warwickshire border - which may account for the Shakespearian flavour of some of the house names. Apart from a new village hall (1998), courtesy of the

Millennium Commission and the National Lottery, little appears to have changed over the years, save some excellent barn conversions. Lying off the beaten track on a loop lane it still retains some thatched houses and even boasts the novelty of a thatched letter box.

INKBERRROW in contrast is divided by the busy Worcester/Stratford road with the old village now almost overcome by twentieth century expansion. Devotees of the long running radio soap opera *The Archers* may find it of special interest

Thatched letterbox,
Abbots Morton

for one of the inns, The Old Bull, is generally accepted as the inspiration for Ambridge's village pub.

THE WALK

From the church walk through the village and continue on the quiet lane for a further 600 yards. (Note: Alternatively as the village comes to an end, near Tudor Cottage, take the stiled footpath on the left which curves round a cottage and heads eastwards over fields to join the bridleway 200 yards up from the road.)

At a bend in the road go forward towards Morton Spirt Farm, with its sow and piglets weather vane, and turn left on the bridleway. In three-quarters of a mile the way divides. Branch right to a hunting gate and keeping the hedge to your right continue for 600 yards. At a metal gate turn left onto a farm track to meet the lane with Knighton Farm to your right.

Turn left and in a few paces right on a hedged/fenced path to reach a stile in 200 yards and bear right on a wide track to a gate/stile. Bear half left passing a corner of woodland to a footbridge and make towards a point a

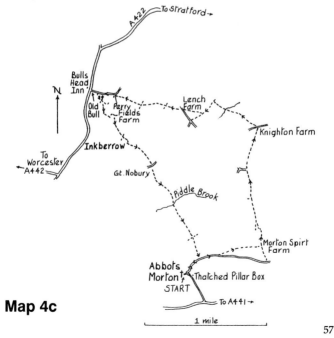

Map 4c

Abbots Morton

little to the left of a solitary tree. Turn left on a bridleway and continue at the top of the field, now hedged on both sides. In about 80 yards take the path on the right heading half left over fields towards Lench Farm.

Cross the lane and bear diagonally right up the slope to a stile. Paths cross here but keep ahead - half left roughly in the direction of the tower seen on a distant hillside and continue over fields to the crest of a hill and the unveiling of the view to Inkberrow church and village.

Descend to a metal gate and forward on a track with Perry Fields Farm to your left and continuing on a lane into Inkberrow. The timber framed "Old Bull" with a friendly looking Herefordshire on its sign is on your left, and ahead is the Bulls Head Inn.

To make the return journey retrace your steps a short distance down the lane and take the churchyard path as far as the tower. Here bear right, down steps and turn left with a small stream. In a short distance cross the stream and then right to the top of an open green and leave by steps near Pepper Street. Turn immediately left descending to Rock Cottage and left to a stile and right along a hedge to cross a footbridge and remain with the path under trees with the stream to your right.

Continue with a hedge to your left and partway down a field and over

58

a stile and on with the hedge to your right. Turn left on a bridleway and in a few yards right up a bank to follow a fenced path. Beyond steps bear left along a hedgerow then descend with it on your right to a stile and over the field to meet a lane.

Follow the Great Nobury drive and 60 yards after crossing a brook take a path on the left to a stile and forward with a hedge to your left, rising and falling, to cross the footbridge over Piddle Brook. Turn right and through a metal gate then left along the field edge. At a stile go ahead but partway up the field the path transfers to the other side of the hedge - resume your direction to a stile. Continue to meet a wide track leading to a farm. At a pond go forward into Abbots Morton by Lilac Cottage.

4d: *Feckenham Wylde Moor and Burial Lane*

Starting Point:	Village car park, off High St, Feckenham
Distance:	Southern loop: 4¼ or 2 miles
	Northern loop: 3 miles or full walk 6¼ miles
Map:	1.50,000 Landranger 150 Worcester & The Malverns
	1.25,000 Explorer 220 Birmingham & Redditch and 205 Stratford-upon-Avon & Evesham for part of southern loop. (Pathfinder 975 Redditch & Henley-in-Arden, Pathfinder 997 Stratford-upon-Avon (West).)

NOTES: Mainly level but rough underfoot in places with some wetlands walking.

FECKENHAM, once the heart of a royal hunting forest, lies on a road the Romans built between the salt town of Droitwich and their camp at Alcester. John Howman, later to be known as John of Feckenham, was born here in 1518. A bright boy of humble origin, educated at Evesham Abbey and Oxford, he became a prominent Roman Catholic preacher and chaplain to Queen Mary I. She was the Bloody Mary of a reign which saw the martyrdom of hundreds of Protestants, notably Bishops Cranmer, Ridley and Latimer. During Mary's five year reign John was made Abbot of Westminster but was deprived of the appointment following her death and suffered a long period of imprisonment in the Tower of London.

South of the village was a bog which stoutly resisted attempts

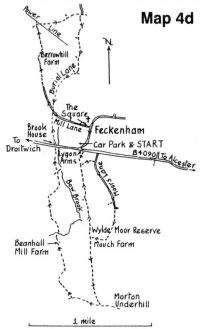

Map 4d

to drain it in the nineteenth century. This is now one of the many nature reserves owned or managed by the Worcester Nature Conservation Trust. It is typical wetland country, soggy underfoot with willow and reed beds to which has been added a pool, a hide open to the public and information board. Beyond the reserve the terrain is one of open farmland, criss-crossed by streams and ditches with long hedgerows which makes good hunting for sparrowhawks and kestrels.

THE WALK -
THE SOUTHERN LOOP
From the car park head down the High Street to the Alcester/ Droitwich road, B4090, and take the path next to the Lygon Arms, signed Bean Hall Mill & Morton Underhill. After crossing a field and a narrow strip of land turn left on a wide track, continuing through allotments. Turn right on the surfaced bridleway of Moors Lane.

In 500 yards the entrance to the Wylde Moor Nature Reserve is found on the right with information board and instructions for reaching the public hide - about 400 yards distant. However continue with the bridleway. When this swings to the left near Andy's Barn keep forward still on a good track but now a public footpath. A further indicator to the hide is met - if visiting take the path that runs close to the main track to reach the hide and pool in about 200 yards.

Retrace your steps and carry on with the hard track to the entrance to Mouch Farm. Here turn right and forward with a hedge and ditch to your left - soggy progress! Cross a footbridge to a stile.

TO COMPLETE THE SHORT SOUTHERN LOOP TURN
RIGHT HERE - FOLLOW THE WAYMARKED PATHS
NORTHWARDS TO RETURN TO FECKENHAM.

FOR THE LONGER LOOP - *Turn left at the stile to a metal gate and
through a wet scrubby area. Cross a broad track to a gate and over a large
field. The next field has a good track running along the hedgerow but the
right of way with stiled exit at end is mapped on the other side of the hedge.
Turn right on the bridleway from Morton Underhill. Keep the hedge on
your right throughout the various twists and turns for the next three-
quarters of a mile when Bean Mill Farm is seen beyond the hedge in a sad
state of ruin.*

*Leave the bridleway at the point where it is signed to Bradley Green
and forward to cross the footbridge over Bow Brook - a tributary of the River
Avon. Bear right and in 100 yards left under trees on a track that is wide
enough to have been an old road or drove - this is followed northwards for
500 yards. As Grove House with its windsock is seen ahead bear right with
a hedge to your left and in about 100 yards through a metal gate and on via
the remnants of a hedged way, bearing left to a gate and forward on a
surfaced track to meet and cross the Alcester Road.*

*Take the bridleway by Brook House signed Ham Green and Cruise Hill
which climbs under trees with the brook below. In a quarter of a mile a
further sign is met.*

TO COMPLETE THE SOUTHERN LOOP *turn right signed The
Square to return to the village - descend to and cross the stream by the Mill
and forward on Mill Lane. Turn right at High Street.*

FOR THE NORTHERN LOOP ONLY
*From the car park follow village street to the Alcester Road and turn right
at Brook House take the bridleway signed Ham Green and continue as
described to Berrow Hill.*

CONTINUATION OF FULL WALK
*Take the bridleway signed Berrow Hill. In 300 yards leave it as it swings
left, and go ahead on a footpath on a greenway between hedges. Cross the
drive of Berrow Hill House passing the buildings to your right to a
waymarked stile and forward over the field to a stile. Cross the top edge of*

a paddock and over a farm drive to a stile, bearing right on a further drive and along a hedgerow with a cottage to your right. Soon swing left keeping the hedgerow to your right to descend a large field.

Bear right with the hedge on your left passing under power lines. In 300 yards the path swops to the other side of the hedge via a plank bridge - maintain your direction ie., eastwards. Keep ahead at the stile and with the hedge to your left go over a further field to meet and turn right on Burial Lane. This is followed for three-quarters of a mile, mostly hedged on both sides. (Should you encounter towards dusk any black clad coffin carrying characters doff your hat and keep quiet.)

When the junction with the outward journey is met turn left signed The Square, descending to cross Bow Brook, passing The Old Mill House and continuing with Mill Lane to The Square where turn right to return to the car park via the High Street.

5
Droitwich

If Kidderminster is synonymous with carpets, Redditch with needles and Worcester with porcelain then the word for Droitwich is salt. An essential but humble commodity although not always an inexpensive item and one on which the town's prosperity was

Salt panning - Droitwich town sign

founded. The history of the salt trade in the town is longer than all the products of its neighbours put together.

At first the salt was easily found - bubbling up to the surface in springs, no doubt discovered as a rime developed as the sun dried the edges of small pools. Later it was pumped to the surface - one such wellhead can be seen near the town centre. The Romans settled here and called the town Salinae. As a measure of the mineral's importance at one time legionaries were paid in salt - *salarium* the soldiers' salt money - thus the derivation of salary. Such was the value of salt that other expressions came into the language. Sitting close to the salt indicated a favoured position at the top table; not worth his salt suggested a man giving poor value to his employer. Many superstitions are connected with salt - spilling it brings bad luck and sprinkling it in a coffin was said to ward off the devil.

Apart from flavouring food, salt was an important preservative in a time when many farm animals had to be killed off as winter approached due to lack of fodder. It was important in pickling, curing ham, with ships' crews relying on barrels of salted beef and pork during long voyages. It had many uses - cleansing wounds, soot and salt made a poor man's toothpaste and it was a useful abrasive.

Hundreds, probably thousands, of years before the Romans came to exploit the mineral resources of Britain, salt was being "exported" from Droitwich to the hillforts of Worcestershire, Gloucestershire and beyond. The product was as vital to everyday life as the flint tools which were traded over great distances. Packaging was as important then as it is now, with clay pots used for the purpose - the first salt cellars! Well before the Norman Conquest a network of Salt Ways had been developed with strings of pack ponies wending their way to all points of the compass - every Wyche Way you might say. Many of these ancient tracks remain today, some as major roads, like the A38 in Worcestershire or the quiet lanes and grassy tracks which still cross the Cotswolds. Numerous references remain - Saltersgate, Salt Way, Salters Lane and the like.

At the time of the Domesday survey the value of salt produced

Severn Valley Railway, Kidderminster

Hanbury church - "Archer weddings" location
The Old Spa Buildings Tenbury - before restoration

Château Impney, Droitwich

at Droitwich was greater than any other in the kingdom. Salt continued to provide employment, a good living for many and a fortune for a handful of owners. Even the church was involved. About AD750 the Mercian King, Ethelbald, gave land to the community at Worcester to build salt houses and furnaces. One of the most famous names in the industry in later times was John Corbett (1817-1901), a local benefactor and apparently a considerate employer. Known as The Salt King, Corbett was also deeply involved in the development of Droitwich as a spa town. It was Corbett who brought the majesty of French stately home architecture to the English midlands with the building of Château Impney, a magnificent mansion in parkland on the edge of the town, now an hotel and conference centre.

Droitwich, or Droitwich Spa as it prefers to be known, has an illustrated town sign showing a man "boiling down". The process became more industrialised with a large area devoted to the trade along the canal in the town centre. Distribution was a problem - pack ponies and carts were insufficient to meet a growing demand

and restricted the expansion of trade. A scheme to build a pipeline from the town to the Severn near Hawford was mooted but came to nothing. The town's river, the meandering Salwarpe, was pressed into service with several locks being built shortly after the restoration to the throne of Charles II but proved to be of limited value and was abandoned in a few years. Much more successful was the barge canal of 1771 which provided the sought-after 7 mile link to the "King's Highway of the Severn" as it was once called.

Apart from the obvious export of the town's major product the canal had an added benefit - the import of large quantities of coal from the South Shropshire collieries around Ironbridge to keep the furnaces going and reducing the cost of production. An old photograph *circa* 1900 shows two large sea-going vessels at the wharf in the centre of Droitwich. By the mid-nineteenth century a further but narrow beam canal of just under 2 miles had been completed to make a junction with the Worcester & Birmingham Canal at Hanbury.

The unrelenting advance of the railway age led to the inevitable decline of the waterways. Happily the Droitwich Canal is now under restoration, supported by the local and county council, a process which may be speeded up by lottery money. The logical inclusion of the Junction Canal in the scheme should provide yet another attractive circuit for waterway cruising and walkers alike.

The Brine Baths at Droitwich opened in 1836, with a salt content said to be ten to twelve times that of the sea - you couldn't actually walk on water but sinking was not much of a hazard. A pleasure that can still be enjoyed today following the reopening in 1985. The production of salt moved away from the town to a site on the Birmingham & Worcester Canal at Stoke a few miles to the north-east. It was here in the early 1920s that an industry dating from prehistoric Britain finally came to an end. In 1998 the story of salt was further commemorated in the town centre by an attractive bronze depicting in graphic detail a group of salt workers at their labours.

A former Member of Parliament for Droitwich, Richard Coote (1636-1701), of Irish descent and an enthusiastic supporter of William III (William of Orange), was in receipt of various honours and appointments. He was Governor of New York and, in 1695, Governor of New England. Pirates, customs dodgers and the like were making inroads on legitimate trade and no doubt the collection of taxes. He determined to suppress this threat and was involved in supplying a ship and financing a certain Captain Kidd who was vested with the authority to detain the pirates. To his chagrin he was more than a little late in discovering that Kidd was himself a notorious pirate. The Governor summoned Kidd to a meeting under some kind of truce but he was arrested and sent back to London, tried for piracy and hung. The mystery of Kidd's considerable fortune in buried treasure remains unsolved to this day.

5a: Hanbury Park and Canal

Starting Point:	Astwood Lane canal bridge (as distinct from Astwood Bridge). Bridge 40, Worcester & Birmingham Canal.
	Location: minor road 1 mile south-east of M5, junction 5
	Limited road edge parking.
Distance:	4¹⁄₂ or 3³⁄₄ miles
Map:	1.50,000 Landranger 150 Worcester, The Malverns
	1.25,000 Explorer 204 Worcester & Droitwich Spa (Pathfinder 974 Droitwich).

NOTES: Mainly level walking. Much of the route is through pasture and parkland - sheep and cattle grazing.

HANBURY church occupies a commanding position looking over its scattered parish from a 340 feet high promontory. It is well known for its connections with the long running radio soap opera *The Archers*. Publicity photographs were shot here for at least two weddings - that of Grace to Phil Archer - a lifetime ago but still well remembered - and of another generation, Lizzie and Nigel Pargetter. The church is much visited by walkers, with a generous array of seats in the churchyard from which to admire the view in comfort. The churchwarden, Mr. J. Spencer, who has a fund of stories about the church, tells me that they can arrange teas for groups of 20 or more given prior notice.

What you see today is mainly a result of eighteenth and nineteenth century work but its origins are much older with elements from the thirteenth century. Like so many of our hilltop churches it

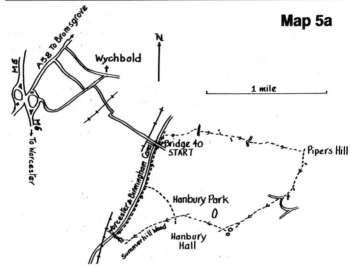

Map 5a

occupies an ideal defensive site - one too good to ignore by hillfort dwellers, you might think, but no definite connection seems to have been established. A monastic foundation is recorded here early in the ninth century.

One of the church's incumbents in 1537, Rowland Taylor, was destined to meet an unhappy end. A barrister and prominent in church affairs he was also a noted preacher. At one time he was domestic chaplain to Archbishop Cranmer and later Chancellor to the Bishop of London, Nicholas Ridley. His strong protestant views and opposition to Mary Tudor, "Bloody Mary", led to his arrest. Like his two more famous fellow clergymen, he was burnt at the stake in 1555.

There are a number of memorials to members of the Vernon family, notably a somewhat overblown monument to Thomas Vernon (1654-1721). A distinguished and leading barrister of the time he was made a Freeman of the City of Worcester in 1715 and served as its Member of Parliament from that time until his death.

His cousin Bowater Vernon's elegiac memorial describes him as enjoying " ...an opulent fortune without pride and regulated his expenses with a wise economy if you except his charities, in which if it were possible he was liberal even to profusion...".

Thomas built HANBURY HALL in 1701 apparently from the proceeds of his lucrative legal career. A handsome red brick house in the grand style with some fine painted ceilings and set in extensive parkland, it is now in the care of the National Trust.

The Worcester & Birmingham Canal is described in the Introduction. At the lock cottage where this walk starts I once saw a notice reflecting the human face of British Waterways - it read "Please do not let the swan into the lock, her mate has been injured by a boat whilst in the lock. We hope to have him back soon. BW." Worcester has a very active Swan Rescue Group which has done sterling work in caring for these stately birds on both the canals and the River Severn.

THE WALK

Take the canal towpath passing the Lock Cottage and in about 150 yards join a field path crossing three fields with the boundary to your right. Leave to join a lane by the epitome of a blasted oak. In an advanced stage of decrepitude, it is a testament to the survival instinct. Half the trunk is missing and what remains is but a hollow blackened shell. Seemingly with only the bark holding it together, it still manages to produce leaves and acorns.

Turn right for a few paces then take the path on the left following the hedgeline to your left. At the end of this long field, cross a farm lane and go forward again. Towards the top of the field bear left over a stile and bridge and then right along the field margins to reach a stile which leads into Pipers Hill Wood.

Go forward a few steps then turn right on clear track which follows the inside edge of the broadleaved wood. Keep forward when a wider track is met by a large oak with a house to your right. Continue beyond a metal gate and wooden kissing gate, climbing to Hanbury church seen ahead.

Leave the church by the tower end gate and head down the lane. Bear right at the junction to take the path on the left into the National Trust's Hanbury Park estate. Go ahead on a diagonal course to stile and on under an avenue of mature oaks. When a metalled drive by a large pool is met swing right heading across the parkland to a point just below a small plantation. Continue to a stile with Brick Kiln Pool seen to your right.

Go directly ahead over further parkland to meet a gate and stile by a further pond. (At this point a path is signed off to the right taking an elliptical course over the fields to join the canal towpath at Astwood Bottom Lock, where turn right. This will shorten the route by about half a mile.) Otherwise keep ahead on a farm track soon passing Summerhill Wood on your left.

As Summerhill Farm is reached swing right, leaving the buildings to your left to reach a path by a canal bridge. Turn right to follow the towpath for a mile along the reed fringed canal where herons may be seen. A popular and peaceful stretch with anglers hopeful of landing roach, carp or perch. Continue past lock 17, Astwood Bottom Lock - narrow gauge and a tight fit in length as well as breadth. At the next lock, return to the road and your starting point.

5b: *Along the Droitwich Canal*

Starting Point:	Salwarpe Church. There is space for a few cars beyond the canal bridge. Salwarpe is 2 miles south-west of Droitwich and signed from the A38 (Worcester Road) at the Trotter Hall Hotel.
Distance:	4¼ miles
Map:	1.50,000 Landranger 150 Worcester, The Malverns
	1.25,000 Explorer 204 Worcester & Droitwich Spa (Pathfinder 974 Droitwich).

NOTES: Towpath, lanes and field paths, mostly level.

The DROITWICH CANAL, still under restoration, is a quiet backwater - the sort to dream about on a lazy summer afternoon; still waters and the restful hum of insects rather than the insistent chug of an outboard motor. A kingfisher may be seen. At Porters Mill I was told of a peregrine raiding a chicken run and of four young red kites perched on the roof top of a Tudor Barn. The kite, once a common bird, was close to extinction, but careful conservation measures in mid-Wales have rescued it. In recent years a release programme to restore the soaring bird of prey to areas it once inhabited (but not London(!) where it was a city scavenger) seems to be proving successful. (Note a forked tail helps to distinguish it from the increasingly common buzzard which is also found in Worcestershire.) That marvellous sight - a skein of geese, or swans in full flight may also be enjoyed.

At SALWARPE the canal flows through a deep and somewhat dark cutting, crowded by trees. It may look its best on one of those mornings when a light mist still clings to the water and veiled reflections paint an ephemeral picture that the artist captures so much better than the camera.

` Salwarpe was the birthplace of Richard de Beauchamp (1382-1439), Earl of Warwick. Like his father, Thomas, he was a soldier in times when disputes were often settled by force of arms rather than legal argument. He fought for Henry IV, with successes against Owen Glendower and at Shrewsbury against the rebel forces of Sir Henry Percy (Shakespeare's Harry Hotspur). He supported Henry V at home and abroad, put down a Lollard rising and when the king's infant son came to the throne Richard was appointed one of his guardians. Today he lies in some splendour in the impressive Beauchamp chapel of St. Mary's Collegiate church in Warwick.

A more modern local hero, and a man of the cloth, was Arthur Douglas. A missionary son of the Rector of Salwarpe, he died in Africa - shot as he attempted to defend some native girls from being raped in 1911.

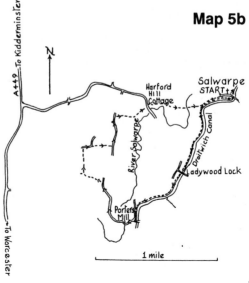

Map 5b

THE WALK

Take the path through the churchyard which falls to the canal bank and turn right on the towpath with intermittent views to an attractive countryside of farms and woodland. In just under a mile Ladywood Lock is met. Here, at the Lock Cottage, a narrowboat may be hired for a half or whole day. Until restoration is completed it is necessarily a short but attractive cruise. (Enquiries: Droitwich Canal Company 01905 458352 - the boat moored nearby has the privileged No. 1 painted on its side.)

From the lock cross the lane and continue with the towpath. Further rebuilt locks are passed although a section in between, thick with reed, awaits the attentions of the dredger's crew. You may notice a waymark for the Monarchs Way - a ship and Charles II taking refuge in the Boscobel Oak. Half a mile from Ladywood, a lane is met. Bear left with it to Porters Mill.

A sign at the canal bridge directs walkers along the towpath to Hawford Mill but our route swings right on Porters Mill Lane.

There was a mill here when William the Conqueror's great inventory of the wealth of the nation, the Domesday book, was compiled in 1086. For many centuries it ground corn; later it was used to clean seed and grain - the winnowing process. The present mill, a large brick building, now a private residence, dates from 1886. Two 12 feet undershot wheels provided the power on one side and a further wheel can just be seen over the wall on the other side. The Salwarpe was once locked, maybe with flash locks: when it was necessary to close the lock to divert the flow into the mill leat, the fields around were flooded.

The need for more working space led to what appears to have been an ambitious piece of engineering with a long drive shaft connected to machinery in the barn by Mill Hall. The Hall, once called Tappenhall, is a fine jettied, timber framed building, with five Tudor chimneys. It carries its age well. Queen Elizabeth spent three days here on a journey through the county. The timbers of the adjacent barn are said to have come from Tewkesbury bridge after the battle of 1471. Bloody Meadow remains in that town today to mark the great slaughter which took place there in yet another battle for the English throne.

Continue past the mill, over the Salwarpe bridge, following the rising lane for half a mile. At a wisteria covered brick house take the wide track on the left. This gives a forward view to the distant Woodberry Hill. Crowned by the trees that hide the hill fort, this is where Owen Glendower and Henry IV's army had a brief skirmish - no more than a Mexican stand-off.

In 300 yards curve right with the bridleway to reach a narrow lane in a quarter of a mile. Turn right and in 100 yards take the path on the right, over a short field (view to the long silhouette of the Malvern Hills to the south). At the next field keep ahead with the hedge to your right. At a stile continue, now with the hedge to your left. Exit by a stile along a short stretch of hedged path and turn left on a lane.

Curve right at a road junction and in 100 yards take the path on the right along the edge of a short then long field. The next field is crossed on a diagonal left course to meet a lane by a bridge over the River Salwarpe. Turn left and in a short distance turn right on a good track by Harford Hill Cottage, signed Salwarpe ³/₄ mile. In a quarter of a mile take the signed path on the right, between a hedge thick with blackthorn and bramble and a wire fence. At a stile take a waymarked course, eastwards over a rising field, to meet and cross the footbridge over the Salwarpe. Here the Environment Agency have a flume - a water flow measurement station.

Cross the field to climb the short bank opposite. Keep ahead with the canal almost hidden below to your right. The large brick mansion seen a mile to your left is Westwood Park which features in the next walk. The path, via a succession of stiles, will bring you back to the village road where turn right to your starting point.

5c: Dovedale and Westwood Park

Starting Point:	Doverdale - small car parks by the church. Doverdale is on a minor road, signed off the A449 at Dunhampton - 7 miles north of Worcester
Distance:	4¹/₄ miles
Map:	1.50,000 Landranger 150 Worcester, The Malverns
	1.25,000 Explorer 204 Worcester & Droitwich Spa (Pathfinder 974 Droitwich).

NOTES: Mainly level walking, including a section of the Wychavon Way. Some care required towards the end of the walk as it follows field edges and paths that may not have been "recovered" following ploughing.

DOVERDALE, a tiny rural community, has a small but fine church,

St. Mary's, in sandstone with a leaded steeple, that throws back the light - a good landmark for walkers.

Our walk passes within sight of Westwood House, for centuries the home of the Pakington family. The story of some of their number is one of deep involvement in the politics of both church and state, of loyalty to the crown, of fortunes lost and fortunes regained. John as a family name was handed down from father to son through the generations - a brief resumé of some of the more interesting episodes in their very full lives will serve to illustrate an eventful dynasty which would not disgrace one of today's period dramas.

The Pakington's home was first at nearby Hampton Lovett and later at Westwood. Sir John Pakington, who died in 1560, was a lawyer during the reign of Henry VIII. It was the king who gave him Westwood. Sir John was active in Welsh matters. In 1540 he was assigned to investigate the "disappearance" of jewellery and other valuable offerings made at the Pembrokeshire cathedral shrine of St. David.

His successor, Sir John of course (1549-1625), built much of Westwood House and had a reputation for extravagance. It was he who added the Great Pool in Westwood Park with scant regard to other people's boundaries. Measuring roughly 800 by 500 yards it held a considerable quantity of water. When the inevitable complaints persisted, Sir John, in a fit of pique, had the banks torn down and flooded the neighbourhood.

Sir John Pakington (1620-1680) was an ardent supporter of the monarchy and Member of Parliament for Worcester from 1639 but his adherence to Charles I was soon to cost him his seat. He fought against the Parliamentarian army in the first full scale battle of the Civil War, at Edge Hill in 1642. Following the royalists defeat after bitter years of fighting, he was ordered to appear before the House of Commons and was fined the value of one third of his estate. He failed to pay the penalty which had been imposed and suffered the temporary loss of his estates which produced the desired effect.

In August 1651 the young Charles marched south to Worcester with his Highland army and was proclaimed King in the City's Guildhall. Pakington joined him at Pitchcroft, contributing to the cavalry forces being assembled on the racecourse. Unfortunately he had backed the wrong side again. A bloody battle to the south of the city and in the city streets on the 3rd of September ended with the king narrowly escaping and Pakington one of many prisoners. His estates were again forfeit. Troubles never come singly, especially if you are the author of your own fate. In 1654, Pakington together with the High Sherrif of Worcestershire, Sir Henry Lyttleton, were accused of accumulating arms and languished in the Tower of London until September 1655. Four years later Sir John's estates were once more forfeited, for his alleged involvement in the rising of Sir George Booth against Cromwell's Protectorate. The restoration of the monarchy in 1660 restored the family fortunes. Sir John was believed to have received a secret award of £4000 for his loyalty, it being recorded under the pseudonym of Edward Gregory. He was again returned as MP for Worcester, holding the seat until 1679.

It was popularly supposed that Sir John Pakington (1671-1721) was the model for the writer and politician Joseph Addison's, Sir Roger de Coverley. Following the family tradition he too was MP for Worcester from 1690. He was involved in much acrimony with the Bishop of Worcester, William Lloyd, and took the matter to the House of Commons. The Bishop and others had accused the MP of profanity, immorality, drunkenness and other matters. The House took the view that the Bishop had been "malicious ... unchristian... in high violation of the liberty and privilege of the Commons ..."

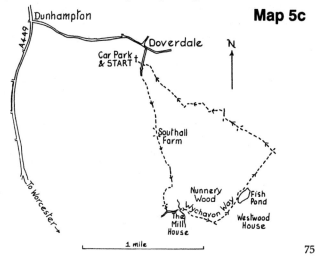

Map 5c

and succeeded in a petition to Queen Ann to have the Bishop removed from his post as Lord Almoner.

The walk encompasses a mix of woodland, arable and pasture through a gently undulating landscape - ideal buzzard country - you are almost certain to see a pair at any time of the year. In summer you may even see a whole family enjoying the thermals that carry them spiralling effortlessly high over their hunting grounds. It is at this time that your attention may be attracted by their mewing calls - not quite the sound you might at first associate with a predatory bird.

THE WALK

Follow the metalled lane, which becomes a bridleway, southwards from the church. Continue between the buildings of Southall Farm and shortly, onwards beyond a metal gate. At the end of this field pass through the larger of two metal gates and forward. Maintain your direction aiming for the power lines seen directly ahead - about half a mile from Southall Farm.

Beyond a metal gate bear right between the giant robotic legs of the pylons and in 80 yards or so swing left to cross the Hadley Brook and through a wooden gate. The path, an old hollow way, climbs under trees. As the trees open out to provide a window to the world the black and white timber framed buildings of Young's Farm are seen to your right. Worcestershire and Herefordshire are rich in both these and good brick buildings.

On reaching a narrow lane, turn left. You have now joined the waymarked Wychavon Way and will keep company with it for the next mile and a half. At the foot of the hill bear left, but glance to your right to see The Mill House (private residence) which still retains some of its old machinery.

Continue with the bridleway, signed to Hampton, which immediately crosses the swift flowing Hadley Brook. This is a good track and soon bears right following the outside edge of Nunnery Wood with a low heavy, fortress-like, stone wall to your left. Beyond a flight of steps the path climbs with Warren Bank to your right and a view to the ubiquitous Malvern Hills, with the Worcestershire Beacon and North Hill prominent.

About half a mile from The Mill House the path divides. Bear left at first along the outside edge of the wood. Soon Nunnery Farm and the multitude of tall chimneys that crown Westwood House come into view.

The falling path leads to a metal gate - go forward to the gate seen ahead to enter the south-eastern corner of Nunnery Wood. In a few yards a stepped path will be seen on your right - a small diversion to this will reveal the old Fish Pond, now a haven for wildfowl and another almost certain place to see a heron or two.

Retrace your steps and continue, shortly turning right on a broader path which is followed to the wood edge. Continue over a large shapely contoured field, your exit point indicated by two gateposts on the crest of the hill. Keep forward, crossing a path and cattle grid, descending for 300 yards. As a track is noted on your right, leave the Wychavon Way. SWING LEFT (not an obvious path) and the hedgeline should be on your left (no way out if you walk the wrong side). This is where the return to Doverdale needs more careful navigation, and close attention should be given to the OS map and, at present, the rather sparse waymarking.

At the top of the rise the view is to the Woodberry and Abberley Hills. Keep ahead on a grassy way that was once the boundary between two fields, with only a small remnant of hedge remaining. At the foot of the field keep ahead with the hedge to your left. At the top of the field bear right, hedge to your right and soon bearing left with it. Ignore the first small plank bridge almost hidden in the hedgerow. Cross the second, more substantial, footbridge found part way down the field.

Cut half left across this field with Pakington Farm seen to your right. A farm track is crossed, about 200 yards south of the farm and then ahead with the hedge to your left.

At the end of the field, pass through a gap in the hedgerow and swing sharp diagonally right towards a projecting corner and then towards a telegraph pole which carries a waymark. Cross the field at a slight angle, as close to the direction pointed by the waymark as may be practical. You will note from the map the square patch of woodland about 100 yards to your right and the stream rather nearer beyond the hedge on the left. The way (probably no distinct path visible) leads to a footbridge, almost concealed in the field margins.

From the bridge head over the field, your marker point being the telegraph or power line pole seen a little to the south of Doverdale church. At the lane turn right to return to your starting point.

5d: Holt Fleet - The Severn

Starting Point: Holt Fleet bridge - eastern bank. On the A4133 from Ombersley. No formal car parking but it may be possible to leave car by riverside approached by narrow lane at Letterbox Cottage, near caravan site.

Distance: 4¼ miles

Map: 1.50,000 Landranger 150 Worcester, The Malverns

1.25,000 Explorer 204 Worcester & Droitwich Spa (Pathfinder 974 Droitwich).

NOTES: We opted to use quiet lanes for most of the return leg of this walk since they proved to be more practical than the field paths. Several attractive farm and barn conversions will be seen along the way.

Holt Fleet is approached from the east via the attractive black and white village of Ombersley. OMBERSLEY found its way into the pages of history as the first stopping point of King Charles II on his dramatic escape from the Battle of Worcester in 1651.

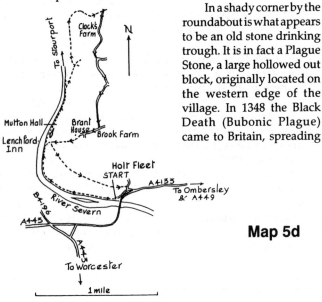

In a shady corner by the roundabout is what appears to be an old stone drinking trough. It is in fact a Plague Stone, a large hollowed out block, originally located on the western edge of the village. In 1348 the Black Death (Bubonic Plague) came to Britain, spreading

Map 5d

across the country with devastating consequences. The Dorset port of Weymouth was one of the early places to be infected, Bristol followed and Gloucester, with its important river connections with Bristol, retreated behind its city walls and ceased trading with the Bristol merchants.

By Christmas the plague had reached London, Parliament suspended its sittings, and those who could left for the countryside - often in vain. A third of the entire population died - perhaps a million people in all, so much so that in some rural areas there were not enough labourers left to work the fields. Villages and towns imposed a form of quarantine, either to keep the plague from its doors or an attempt to prevent the contagion spreading beyond its boundaries. As at Ombersley food and supplies would be deposited at an agreed point and money, often dipped in vinegar, was left in payment.

In the church, St. Andrew's, there are memorials to members of the Sandys family, whose home Ombersley Court can be glimpsed from the graveyard. Here there is a small memorial garden "Given by the people of Worcestershire in memory of Celine Figard whose tragic death was discovered near this place, 29th December, 1995". Celine was a French girl travelling to Hampshire to spend Christmas with a relative, but never arrived. Police investigating her disappearance traced her to the Chievely Services off the M4 near Newbury where she apparently accepted a lift from a lorry driver. The discovery of her body hidden close to a lay-by on the A449 led to one of the biggest murder hunts mounted by West Mercia Police. A long and painstaking investigation which included the checking of the movements of some 12,000 lorries and their drivers eventually led to a successful prosecution.

Walkers following the RIVER SEVERN upstream will probably find it quieter now than at any time in the last five hundred years for this has been one of the most important rivers in England. The navigation of the lower Severn was always a hazardous undertaking with treacherous currents and tides setting traps for the unwary. River pirates further upstream did nothing to reduce the dangers and water levels made matters even more uncertain the further inland one ventured. Travelling downstream on the flood was one thing - the opposite direction often called for hard work. The Severn

Trow, a shallow bottomed vessel which could be sailed or towed by teams of men, known as bow hauliers, solved some of the problems. Ironbridge, the birthplace of the Industrial Revolution, was a particularly busy section of the river with the carriage of locally mined coal and the products of its furnaces.

The 16 mile deepwater canal from Sharpness finally reached Gloucester in 1827. It greatly reduced the dangers of the river passage and allowed larger ships into the port. Gloucester, for centuries a port town, prospered anew, with a large area being developed for docks and warehouses. From here cargoes were offloaded for onward transmission upriver by smaller boats and barges.

The construction of the 42 mile, 5 locks, Severn Navigation from Gloucester northwards to Stourport improved river traffic for the port towns on the route but diminished the activity further upstream. Today there is little or no commercial traffic above the Severn Bridge save the grain barges that come to the Flour Mills at Tewkesbury.

The old time Severn sailors would have grown accustomed to many strange sights on the river but you may encounter one they surely never saw. The distant beat of a drum - it's a weird sound in winter - may herald the arrival of a long dragon boat paddled by a large crew with great discipline at an impressive speed.

THE WALK

The walk starts on the eastern bank of the river by Thomas Telford's single span iron bridge of 1828. This is also the start of the Wychavon Way but take the opposite direction - upstream soon to reach the lock. A wooden kissing gate leads to a path which passes several wooden chalets - riverside retreats, probably built in the 1930s, the like of which can be found at a number of points along the Severn. Continue, with pasture to your right and further chalets and mobile homes lining the opposite bank, each with their attendant moorings, bobbing boats and the occasional nodding fisherman, until a powerful punctuation mark, The Lenchford Inn, brings the settlement to a full stop.

From here the path edges a caravan site, moorings and a quiet pool which provides a sanctuary from the swifter waters of the river for wildfowl. This area is rather too well decorated with Private Land and Keep to the Path notices - perhaps necessary but it does seem very unfriendly in this peaceful spot.

Continue, passing the three gabled, white painted Mutton Hall and soon on a wide track at first under trees. About a quarter of a mile from the Hall, leave the riverbank, following the track up the slope towards woodland. (If you wish to shorten the walk a little continue to the top of the rise and turn right at The Hollies.)

As the woodland is met turn left over a plank bridge and forward along field edges to reach a rough lane in just over a quarter of a mile. Bear right, climbing to meet a three-way junction of lanes. Bear right on the lane, passing Clack's Farm and, by The Granary, a pet cemetery with the occasional bunch of flowers. (At exactly this point a self-satisfied looking white cat carrying a large mouse in its mouth crossed my path - not I think, a funeral procession.)

At a T junction by The Hollies take the lane signed Ombersley. At Carpenters Farm bear right with the lane, and right again at a T junction by Brook Farm. As the lane swings left, keep ahead signed to Mutton Hall, soon passing Brant House. The way dips to pass several mobile homes beyond which a path is signed on the left by a wooden gate.

From this point you have the option of descending to the river and following it downstream to your starting point. Alternatively swing immediately left following field edges for three-quarters of a mile, at first under trees then at the foot of a steep bank thick with gorse and broom - a wildlife haven above which buzzards fly.

A stile leads to a caravan park and on to a narrow lane. Turn right with this to return to your starting point.

6
The Teme Valley

When we move to the Teme Valley we are in hop country with the old oasthouse chimneys giving the impression to visitors from the south that they have unaccountably taken a wrong turning and are back in Kent. Not that they are called oasthouses in Worcestershire, they are hop kilns, and to pursue the point a little further we should speak of hop yards rather than fields. The industry, which dates

Hop vines close to harvest time

back to the mid-seventeenth century, has changed in many respects. The area under crop has been much reduced and at the specially built market in Worcester it's now a case of shops, not hops. No longer do crowds of people from the Black Country and Birmingham spend a paid holiday hop picking for the harvesting and processing is now less labour intensive.

William Cobbett was in Worcester in late September 1826 in the course of his "Rural Rides" and commented on the hop harvest which had been particularly good that year. He refers to the pride in their produce of the growers who clearly felt that the Worcestershire hop had no rival. More jealous of the hop than of their wives and mistresses is how he puts it. Cobbett, usually a blunt man, tactfully refrained from advancing the argument that hops grown in his native Surrey were commanding twice the price of the Worcester crop. The following day he rode into the Teme Valley to visit Sir Thomas Winnington at Stanford Park and was sufficiently impressed to describe the area as one of the finest spots in England. Writing in his host's library (at six o'clock in the morning) he reports that this was one of the best stocked private libraries he had ever seen. Moreover Sir Thomas had actually read the books! There's more - including an enthusiastic description of the landscape and the sporting facilities.

Apart from hops the low-lying land around the river accommodates pasture, with orchards on the slopes of the higher ground and the summits well wooded. Here one must wonder what horrors lie behind the place names - Witchery Hole, Death's Dingle, Devil's Den and Hell Hole.

The River Teme rises in Wales on the slopes of Bryn Coch near the western end of the ancient Kerry Ridgeway. Its course crosses and recrosses the boundary between England and Wales until it reaches Knighton - "the town on the dyke" - Offa's Dyke that is. At Ludlow it flows under the ancient Ludford Bridge, a wide shallow torrent tumbling over a rocky bed where the electric blue flash of a kingfisher is often seen. It enters Worcestershire near TENBURY WELLS, a more mature lowland river after its swifter progress through Powys and Shropshire although it still flows at quite a pace and wide enough to require a six arched bridge. Thence it makes its way through a well wooded landscape of rolling hills with hop fields, orchards and sheep pasture. Tenbury, an old market and coaching town, had aspirations to join the ranks of the prosperous spas. Encouraged by the presence of mineral springs a pump room was built but the customers were slow in coming and the venture failed. The sad remains of a spa building could be seen behind the Crow Hotel near the junction of Market Street and Teme Street. In 1998 English Heritage came to the rescue with a restoration plan. Tenbury can boast something unique - in late November and early December it holds the only Mistletoe Market in Britain.

The Teme, in one of its more serious floods, swept away part of the church in 1770. Within there is a most attractive, almost theatrical gallery, with the continuity of worship preserved in a fragment of an Anglian cross of circa AD880. A handsome table tomb with the effigies of Thomas Acton and his wife who died in 1546 has a Shakespearian connection, for his daughter Joyce married Sir Thomas Lucy of Charlcote Park in Warwickshire. It was Sir Thomas who, it is said, prosecuted the young bard for deer poaching and supposedly is the model for Mr Justice Shallow.

In Teme Street, no. 18, a small plaque commemorates Dr. Henry Hill Hickman, "the earliest pioneer of anaesthesia by inhalation experiment and practised in this building...". Several old inns remain: the Ship not far from the river was a seventeenth century coaching inn and in Market Street the Royal Oak's timber framed upper storeys are now arthritically twisted. Nearby is the Market House, 1811, built in the round with the stalls within similarly and attractively constructed.

SHELSLEY WALSH has long been famous in the world of motor sport for its testing hill climb, and the roar of throbbing engines if not the pounding hearts of competitors may be heard by walkers in the area. The church, St. Andrew's, has an enclosed family pew and to the left of the altar is the wood-panelled tomb of Sir Francis Walsh and his wife Alice. His son, Sir Richard, was High Sheriff of the county at the time of the Gunpowder Plot, 1605, and was involved in the arrest of some of the conspirators. An intricately carved oak rood beam carries a line of candles.

CLIFTON UPON TEME, despite its name, stands on a hill, well back from the river with houses from several centuries. In the church porch there is an elderly wheeled funeral bier above which is a copy of the charter granted to Roger de Mortimer in 1270 by Henry III. Free Borough status is conferred upon Clifton "for ever and the men of the same borough to be free burgesses as other burgesses of our kingdom". A weekly Thursday market and a four day fair were granted. Entry to the church is via a door with an enormous inverted heart shaped handle - the pride of a local blacksmith. In the Woodmanton chapel is the effigy of Sir Ralph Wyesham, Steward of the King's Household and Justice of North Wales, who died in 1332.

LEIGH near Bransford has a remarkable barn - a huge cruck

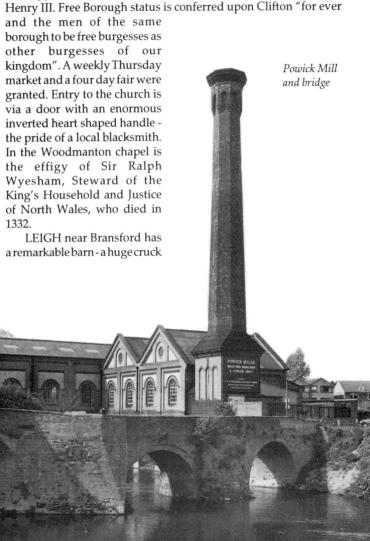

Powick Mill and bridge

framed construction built 600 years ago for Pershore Abbey. Now in the care of English Heritage the building is a silent commentary on the staying power of oak, the skill of the carpenters who built it and the one time wealth of the monastic foundations. Bransford lost its bridge during the Civil War and the crossing at Powick was partly destroyed. Behind it stands the mills that were the site of the first practical sized hydroelectric scheme in Britain.

Away from the main road the explorer of the Teme valley will find himself following a tangle of twisting narrow lanes which wind up and down steep hillsides. The views are superb with farms and villages dotted about a large landscape. Some, with justification, will claim this as the very best of the Worcestershire countryside.

6a: *Pudfoot Hill and the Worcestershire Way*

Starting Point:	Ham Bridge, 9 miles north-west of Worcester via the A443 and B4204 and 1¹/₂ miles beyond Martley. A small parking area is found a little beyond eastern side of the bridge.
Distance:	4 miles
Map:	1.50,000 Landranger 138 Kidderminster & Wyre Forest
	1.25,000 Explorer 204 Worcester & Droitwich Spa
	(Pathfinder 973 Great Witley).

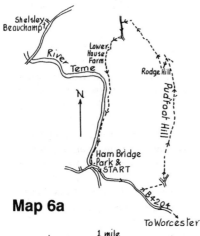

Map 6a

This route follows part of the Worcestershire Way along a 590 feet high ridge with fine views. Below red brick farmhouses, echoing the colour of the red-brown soil, are set amidst the lower fields from which rise partially wooded hills. On a day when stiff breezes encourage a game of hide and seek between fast moving clouds and the sun, the play of light upon the landscape below is an added pleasure. The woodlands provide cover for pheasants which are found in some abundance - even, it is said, a white variety, presumably an albino mutation. Buzzards too find this countryside to their liking and are almost certainly to be seen soaring high above the fields with their accustomed grace and ease. A long view up the valley carries the eye to the hills of south Shropshire. The 1750 feet Titterstone Clee Hill, 15 miles to the north-west, may be identified by the glint of sun on the giant golf ball of the satellite earth navigational station.

THE WALK

From the car park area head along the road away from the bridge shortly passing Hambridge Farm. Ignore the southbound Worcestershire Way on the right. Two hundred yards beyond the farm take the signed path on the left to follow a grassy tread up a hillside dotted with birch trees to a stile. Head slight diagonally right with The Tee Farm seen forward. Its pond is noisy with ducks and some Hawaiian geese, the famous Ne-Ne, may be seen. While the public footpath passes close to the ponds they are actually on private land which should of course be respected.

A stile leads into a larch plantation. Head very slight left to a stile and then left. Bear right as the track joins a metalled lane and almost immediately left up a stepped bank into woodland. Ignore the first left turn and continue, initially in parallel with the road, through a wooded area with the hill falling sharply away.

The path emerges into the open to provide some splendid views which may be partly restricted by new plantations. Maintain your direction along the crest of Pudfoot Hill with the fence and trees to your right. Continue passing through gateways and crossing the bridleway which has wound up the hillside from Pudfoot Farm. Midway over the next field a seat has been placed here as a gesture of thanks to those who worked on the Worcestershire Way.

About 250 yards beyond the seat the path dips to a prominent Worcestershire Way signpost. Here fishhook left through a metal gateway on a gently descending track by a plantation and on towards mature woodland. Beyond a green gate go ahead on the inside of the wood. Just short of the point where a house is seen ahead leave the Worcestershire Way (which now turns up the hillside) and continue towards the house to join a track.

Keep ahead to pass a pool overlooked by a Cedar of Lebanon. Beyond the pool leave the track at a bend and take the path on the left which climbs to meet a narrow farm lane by a large house. Turn left with the lane with a view ahead to the great black bulk of the northern end of the Malvern Hills looming up in the distance. Keep with the lane as it descends to Lower House Farm with the neat sandstone church at Shelsley Beauchamp seen beyond the orchards to your right.

The farm has a collection of fine mellow red brick buildings with matching tiles dulled by lichen and a large barn punctured by a patterning of ventilation holes. The right of way as shown on my edition of the map does not appear to be easily accessible but enquiries at the farm confirmed that it is in order to proceed with the main buildings to your right to the metal gateway. (Watch for signs or waymarks in case of any change.) Swing half left to the field gate seen in the opposite hedge.

Beyond the hedge bear left along the field margin to cross a stream - no bridge. In wet weather care may be needed to find a suitable crossing point. Go forward to pass through a gateway. Ignore the path on the left and continue on the inside edge of woodland, soon with the gleam of the Teme seen below.

In 200 yards bear right with the boundary curving downhill to emerge into a field. Go ahead with the wooded area to your left towards a line of willows and cross a small stream. Now take a diagonal course over the field to follow the banks of the Teme to Ham Bridge where turn left to regain your starting point.

6b: Ankerdine Hill

Starting Point:	Ankerdine Common Picnic Site on the Worcestershire Way. 9 miles west of Worcester - take A44 and turn right on B4197 as Knightsford Bridge is reached. Sharp right at Tower Cottage half a mile after Knightwick church.
Distance:	4 miles
Map:	1.50,000 Landranger 150 Worcester, The Malverns
	1.25,000 Explorer 204 Worcester & Droitwich Spa (Pathfinder 995 Bromyard).

NOTES: This is a strenuous walk with some steep ascents and wet patches in woodland.

The first leg of this walk explores the Worcestershire Way northwards and is well waymarked with the black pear logo. The route provides many good views and is particularly recommended for a late autumn day which adds great splashes of vivid colour in counterpoint to the dark smudges of more distant hills. Apart from the woodland and the connecting lanes much of the walk is through sheep pasture and some fine Herefordshire cattle may be seen around the Horsham area. Again this is ideal buzzard country.

Knightwick and the Talbot Inn have found a small place in history as the scene for one of the many stories associated with the escape of Charles II after the battle of Worcester in 1651. The historian John Noake reports that the king travelling in various disguises, both male and female, assumed the role of a shoe black whilst stopping at the inn.

THE WALK

From the picnic site retrace your steps towards the road. As Tower Cottage is reached turn right through a gateway and swing half left down the hillside towards a stile to enter Nipple Coppice. Bear right on a falling path and in 250 yards bear left as waymarked. In 200 yards at a T junction turn

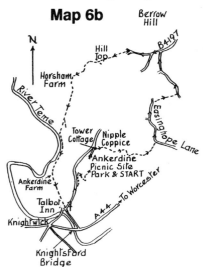

Map 6b

right and in 150 yards sharp left to cross a small stream and stile to emerge into the open. (The stream rises from a spring a little to the north - Nipple Well - which gives the wood its name.)

Ahead is a steep green bank with four oak trees ranged along the slope. Head at a slight right-angle up the hillside to a field boundary. Thence forward with the hedgerow to meet a waymark post. Keep forward on the outside edge of a wood to meet a metal gate and bear left on Easinghope Lane.

The lane is followed past

Hawksnest Farm. At a small crossroad bear right with Easinghope Farm to your left. Ignore the first signed path on the right but 300 yards from the last junction take the path on the right (still with the Worcestershire Way) crossing fields, waymarked and roughly along the course of power lines. In 400 yards meet a narrow lane and turn left. (Note this is the point at which the Worcestershire Way is abandoned.) Follow the lane for 600 yards, ignoring the first left turn. Ahead is Berrow Hill, its tree covered slopes concealing an ancient hillfort.

Turn left as you reach the B4197 and in 150 yards bear right on the lane signed Horsham. In 300 yards by the drive to Old House Farm, leave the road and take the signed and stiled path from which there is a fine view including the red brick Hill Top - quite a picture. Cross the falling field to the far left corner and over a plank bridge. Shortly bear right over a stream and stile and swing left along a hedgerow with Hill Top above you. Ignore the signed path on the left and continue to the end of the field. Bear slight right, soon meeting a waymark post and continuing with a hedgeline to your right. In 100 yards cross a stile on the right heading half left towards Horsham Farm.

Bear left on the farm lane, through a gate and half right between the farm buildings, over a ladder stile into an enclosed area and over a further ladder stile. Go ahead joining a clear track with a long period of level walking.

The track is followed through the fields to reach Ankerdine Farm in three-quarters of a mile. The River Teme provides company for a short distance - so deep beneath its banks that one wonders how it could possibly escape from its allotted course when in flood.

Pass between the buildings of Ankerdine Farm to follow a concrete way, with hop yards on one side and a nursery with pot grown trees and shrubs on the other, to reach the Talbot Inn and the B4197. Turn left passing the neat little Victorian church and the former tiny telephone exchange, now the village hall.

In 400 yards take the Worcestershire Way signed on the right. A steep path winds up the wooded slopes of Ankerdine Hill. When well up the hillside swing right by a waymark post and after a further ascent and steps turn left on a broad track passing a house with an enviable view. A prospect that can soon be shared from the small picnic area on the left.

Continue through a white metal gate to return to your starting point. The extensive views to the east and north include Worcester, 9 miles, with the Glover's Needle more easily identified than the darker tower of the cathedral.

6c: Shelsley Walsh and the Hill Climb

Starting Point: Clifton upon Teme - church.

Distance: 5³/₄ miles

Map: 1.50,000 Landranger 138 Kidderminster & Wyre Forest
1.25,000 Explorer 204 Worcester & Droitwich Spa
(Pathfinder 973 Great Witley).

NOTES: Some steep ascents/descents, boots recommended.

The small and attractive village of Clifton upon Teme occupies the high ground with a good network of paths that ensure that the walker is rarely bereft of extensive views. The route that follows offers a fine prospect of the line of hills that rise above the eastern bank of the Teme, effectively walling off the valley. Overlooking this is the Iron Age fort hidden in the trees of Woodbury Hill and the more open ground of Pudfoot and Rodge Hills traversed by the Worcestershire Way and where buzzards wheel and soar. In the north-east the county's answer to Big Ben, the clock tower in the grounds of Abberley Hall, can scarcely be missed. The north-west

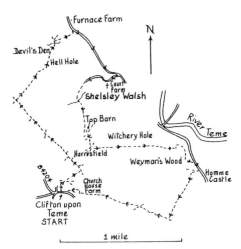

Map 6c

1 mile

leg of the walk, in the first mile, gives a clear view to Shropshire's Titterstone Clee and Brown Clee Hill, both over 1750 feet high. The course of the famous hill climb at Shelsley Walsh, a challenge to sporting motorists since 1905, is walked affording further views. The last long climb back to Church House Farm opens up retrospective views to the Malvern Hills and Bredon Hill backed by the long dark blur of the Cotswold escarpment.

The author is becoming addicted to the Teme Valley - not surprising for the scenery is particularly rewarding. If it were not for the need to provide a balanced picture of walking opportunities in Worcestershire several more circuits would be included.

THE WALK

Take the signed path next to the church which follows the driveway of a house and bear right beyond a gateway and forward. At the end of the field leave by a stile a few yards up the boundary (not the one at the corner). Head half left to follow the field edge to exit by a stile. Keep forward initially with a hedge to your right. Maintain your direction, north-west, for three-quarters of a mile and over fields and a farm track when the hedge is left behind.

When an enclosed bridleway is met turn right and continue beyond a gate over a short field to a further gate. Descend, with the broken line of trees ahead as your marker, to meet and enter woodland.

We are in alien country with a touch of the wild wood - Hell Hole lies to the right and Devil's Den to the left. If this makes you feel uneasy you will not be comforted by the knowledge that Furnace Farm is further on. The way through the wood is not always clearly defined but I see that the Rights of Way team has been busy with its yellow tape, which suggests that waymarking and an improvement in the path may be expected.

A 400 yard descent will bring you to a stream. If you are facing a wide plank bridge do not cross but bear left with the track, soon to cross a culverted stream and bearing right along a fenced area to leave woodland. Follow the fence to a gate and half right to meet the road south of Furnace Farm.

Turn right with the road for half a mile to Shelsley Walsh. Turn right with the tarmac drive signed to the church, passing the open sheds that will house the competition cars. Bear right passing a large house and left to start the long steep ascent of the tarmac hill climb.

At the foot of the hill there is a memorial tablet to Raymond Mays - "1899-1980 Shelsley Walsh was his favourite venue between 1922 and 1950, he made best time of the day on 21 occasions. He was the inspiration and founder of the ERA and BRM".

There is a huge contrast here for this is sheep country but with spring over the maternal bleatings that echo across the fields give way to the deeper notes of straining engines. Yet it doesn't seem out of place. The wooden benches that line the slopes fade into the landscape and only the successive "sentry boxes" of the race officials and the odd tyre wall tell of another activity.

Keep with the course, a private road with access only to pedestrians, continuing beyond the woods to the double metal gates at Top Barn. Go forward on the track to the house at Harrisfield. (Note the walk may be shortened at this point - Clifton is only half a mile distant and there is a choice of waymarked return paths.)

As the house is approached swing left over a field to a stile and continue to a gate that leads into a wood. (Note - not the stile set further along the boundary.) Continue on a broad track but in 100 yards bear left on a waymarked and narrower path, resuming your eastward direction with the steep slopes falling to Witchery Hole to your left. In another 100 yards as the path descends bear right up a bank. This is a narrow secret way with the gleam of the Teme glimpsed through the trees and the deep valley to your left. After a while the path widens and continues under conifers with a steady descent. After curving to the left for 60 yards bear right at a waymarked post, descending to emerge into the open and on to meet the road. Turn right to Homme Castle - 150 yards. (The remains of a motte to the east of the road suggests the origin of its name; today a business centre is housed in the farm buildings.)

Two paths are signed on the right. Take the second which passes through a small enclosure and beyond a short field bear left on the grassy track and continue beyond a gate to the edge of the wood. Ignore the path seen a little to the right and go forward with the hedge to your right to enter a somewhat gloomy wood. Go ahead on a wide track and when back in the open bear right along the woodland edge and forward, briefly under trees. With the hedge to your right now climb steadily (good retrospective views), later levelling out and on a clear track, to reach Church House Farm in three-quarters of a mile.

Bear left at the farm to meet and turn right on the road to return to your starting point.

7
Worcester

In earlier chapters an attempt has been made to give a flavour of the area being explored but a history of Worcester is likely to take more space than it should in a book primarily devoted to walking. It is

Worcester Cathedral from the Severn

hoped that this arbitrarily selected calendar of events and the short town walk that follows will provide at least a sketch for those who do not already know the city. Some of the dates are approximate.

A Worcester Calendar

500 BC	Iron Age village located close to the east bank of the River Severn.
AD100 to 300	Roman fort and settlement. Iron smelting in progress. Fourteen hundred years later the enterprising Andrew Yarranton sends large quantities of the slag up the Severn and the Dick Brook near Shrawley for further refining.
681	The See of Worcester created.
872-899	Worcester fortified, later medieval walls built. Some remains exist today.
961- 965	Oswald (later canonised) is appointed Bishop, is active in reform of the monastic life and establishes Benedictine church, St. Mary's, beside St. Peter's which had been built in the seventh century. Excavations in 1997 in the area of today's Chapter House suggest the early cathedrals were larger than had been thought.
1041	Worcester razed to the ground by Harthacnut following the citizens' resistance to his tax collectors, two of whom were slain. The "tax evaders" escape capture by hiding out on an island in the Severn upstream at Bevere.
1048	Florence of Worcester records that in this year the city suffered from a great earthquake with many casualties.
1066	Bridges over the Severn known to have existed before the Norman Conquest.
1070	Worcester Castle built - it did not survive beyond about 1300.
1084/1085	Bishop Wulstan (later canonised) builds new church/ monastery which becomes cathedral and opens hospital of The Commandery. Later this is purchased by a rich clothier Thomas Wylde who made it his home. Charles II adopts it as his headquarters in 1651.

1088	Worcester comes under attack as rebels attempt to dethrone William Rufus. Bishop Wulstan, now very elderly, takes charge of the defence. The great courage of a handful of men saves cathedral, town and castle from the fire and pillage that affects much of the county. It is hailed as a miraculous deliverance against overwhelming odds that is attributed to Wulstan who promised that if the defenders were valiant they would be unharmed. It is said that the Bishop laid a powerful curse on the attackers that robbed them of both their will and ability to fight.
1113	Worcester burns as a great fire sweeps through the city causing widespread damage including cathedral and castle.
1131	Worcester burns again.
1139	Matilda's forces partly destroy Worcester during the war between Stephen and Matilda.
1175	The new tower of Worcester cathedral falls.
1181	Florence of Worcester, the chronicler, dies.
1189	Worcester is again badly damaged by a great fire. Receives first Royal Charter from Richard I.
1202	Yet another great fire.
1203	Bishop Wulstan who died in 1095 is canonised for his unrelenting work in an unruly era (both religious and secular). He is credited with much good work in the establishment of churches, preaching against the Bristol slave trade and demanding that vows of celibacy be maintained by the priests under his jurisdiction. Pilgrims flock to the cathedral to pay their respects at his shrine.
1210	The year of the great freeze - the Severn is frozen from bank to bank.
1216	King John dies and by his express wish is buried in Worcester Cathedral between the saintly bishops Wulstan and Oswald.
1218	The government of Henry III and the Welsh leader Llywelyn ap Iorwerth agree peace terms known as Treaty of Worcester.

Leigh Court Barn interior - English Heritage
Malvern Priory from the hills

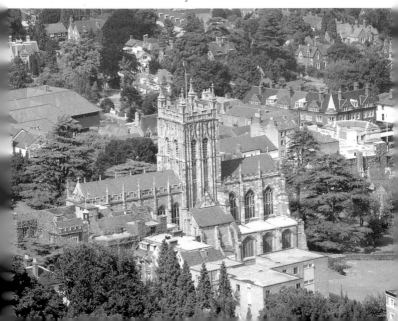

1220	A gale brings down two of the cathedral towers.
1227	Henry III grants charter to establish merchants' guild. Over the years guilds included Glovers & Pursers, Cordwainers & Shoemakers, Bakers, Clothiers, all before 1500, and later Mercers, Tailors & Drapers, Ironmongers, Butchers, Barbers, Tallow Chandlers, Bricklayers, Coopers and Masons.
1263	Worcester plundered following siege at the outbreak of the Barons War.
1264	The Barons War - Pact of Worcester, an offer from Simon De Montfort's administration which the supporters of Prince Edward cannot refuse.
1278	Kings, princes and nobles attend a great celebration as Llewellyn ap Gruffudd, Prince of Wales is married at the cathedral. A short lived marriage, for the bridegroom was killed four years later at Builth Wells when the long running hostilities between England and Wales resumed.
1313	First stone bridge built over the Severn replacing earlier wooden bridges. They built well - it lasted until 1771 when replaced by the present bridge which in turn was restructured in 1931.
1348/49	The dreaded Black Death which killed a third of the population of England reaches Worcester.
1374	Central tower of cathedral, commenced in 1357, completed.
1378	Watergate entrance to cathedral built.
1399	The Welsh under Owen Glendower are in revolt and an attack is made on Worcester.
1467	The playing of tennis within the Guildhall is prohibited. Fire is still a worry to the authorities - wooden chimneys and thatched roofs are banned.
1485	Henry VII, victor at Battle of Bosworth, has Richard III's supporters beheaded in Worcester and city fined.
1502	Prince Arthur heir to the throne of Henry VII and elder brother of the future Henry VIII, dies at Ludlow aged 15

The Glovers Needle - St Andrew's Spire and old warehouses from the river and is buried in a chantry chapel in Worcester Cathedral.

1575   Queen Elizabeth makes a royal progress through Worcestershire and is so impressed by the black pear tree planted to celebrate her visit that the emblem is included in the city's coat of arms.

*c.*1600   City Walls fully complete. Six gates give access.

1642   The Civil War breaks out. A treasure train carrying silver donated to aid the Royalist cause passes through Worcester en route for the King's mint in Aberystwyth. An attack on the wagons by a detachment of Cromwell's Cavalry at Powick Bridge is beaten off by Prince Rupert. Worcester does not fare so well and is obliged to surrender to Parliamentary forces under the Earl of Essex. The unfortunate Mayor is taken into captivity, horses stabled in the cathedral and rich vestments vandalised. The city walls are not in good order and after a period Worcester is abandoned as being impractical to hold and reverts to being garrisoned for Charles. The city suffers under later sustained sieges before a final surrender to Parliament in 1646 at the end of the first stage of the Civil War.

1651   Charles II marches south from Scotland and enters Worcester on 22nd August. On 3rd September the bloody battle of Worcester ends in the Royalist defeat and Charles narrowly escapes capture.

1690   Berrow's Worcester Journal, believed to be the world's oldest newspaper, first published.

*c.*1720   Three Choirs Festival, a major musical event, alternates between the cathedral cities of Worcester, Gloucester and Hereford and continues to this day.

1721   Worcester Guildhall with its impressive frontage to the High Street built.

1725   Daniel Defoe visits the city and reports in his "A Tour Through the Whole Island of Great Britain" that Worcester is large, populous, old though not well built and complains that the houses are too closely crowded together. The cathedral, he says, is both ancient and decayed. Of the people, he says they are considered to be rich, full of business, chiefly with the clothing trade.

1750   Dr. John Wall establishes the Worcester, later Royal Worcester, porcelain factory.

1781   The diarist, John Byng - later Lord Torrington - visits the city; comments unfavourably on the conduct of the cathedral services but praises the "beautiful gothic magnificence of Prince Arthur's Tomb"; visits the porcelain factory - flourishing but again not complimentary. Foregate Street is described as "the ornament of Worcester" and "the city well built and paved". Byng seems to have enjoyed a meal of local salmon and perry.

1815   Worcester & Birmingham Canal opened.

1825   The world famous Worcestershire Sauce begins production at the premises of Lea & Perrins.

1830   William Cobbett's "Rural Rides" is published. He is well pleased with Worcester: "...one of the cleanest, neatest and handsomest towns I ever saw: indeed I do not recollect to have seen any one equal to it". Like Defoe he is less than complimentary about the cathedral. Of the population, they are "most suitably dressed and most decent looking people. The town is precisely in character with the beautiful and rich country in the midst of which it lies". He comments on the immense value of the glove trade to the city and county and the economic advantages of the mix of agriculture and industry.

1834   Shire Hall (Foregate Street), now the Crown Court, built.

1845   Work on the Severn navigation in progress and twin locks completed at Worcester.

1850   Railway comes to Worcester.

1860   Railway extended from Foregate Street to the Severn to service river trade and warehouses.

1851   Salmon fishing continues to provide employment for 74 people from a number of families living in Severn Street near the cathedral.

1857   Edward Elgar (later knighted) born at Lower Broadheath. Before he achieved national and international fame his career included work as a church organist, music teacher, bandmaster at the Powick mental institution and participation in the Three Choirs Festival.

1865   Worcester County Cricket Club inaugurated.

1905   Sir Edward Elgar receives freedom of Worcester

1929   Worcester's centuries old fishing industry brought to an end when netting of salmon is banned.

7a: A Worcester City Walk

Starting Point:	Worcester Bridge.
Parking:	Car parks north of the bridge - Croft Road and Pitchcroft. South of the bridge - Copenhagen Street also accessed from Bridge Street.
Distance:	1¼ miles approx.
Map:	A local street map would be useful but not essential. The sketch map is diagrammatic and not to scale.

NOTES: This is a short walk taking in many of the city's points of interest but is in no way exhaustive. Visiting all the places mentioned will take the best part of a day. For those opting to go directly to a particular point a brief summary follows.

The cathedral is at the far (southern) end of the High Street; Royal Worcester Porcelain lies beyond, off Severn Street. The Commandery - Civil War Centre - is nearby at Sidbury on the A38 just over the canal bridge. The Guildhall is in the High Street, Grey Friars and Tudor House Museum are in Friar Street and King Charles House (now a restaurant) at the foot of New Street.

The main shopping areas are concentrated around the High Street (extending to The Cross) with the Crowngate Centre and open market to the west, Reindeer Court, The Shambles and the Hop Market off the east side. Worcester has a number of antique shops which will be found in the cathedral area and the A38 running north beyond Foregate Street station ie. The Tything and Upper Tything - again not an all embracing list. River trips operate from both North and South Quays on the east bank of the river.

For a guide to opening times please refer to Useful Information.

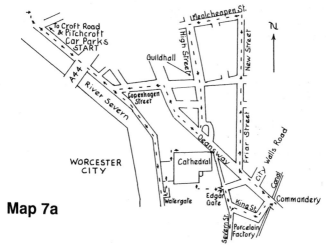

Map 7a

For excellent views over the city from the east two points are recommended. The small park, Fort Royal, the old artillery bastion, gives a particularly fine prospect of the cathedral and to the Malvern Hills - follow Sidbury towards the London Road for a short distance beyond The Commandery and turn left on Wylds Lane and thence right on a steep stepped path. Lansdowne Crescent also offers wide views over the city and northwards. It is reached via Lowesmoor and Lowesmoor Terrace then left from Rainbow Hill.

THE WALK
From Worcester Bridge (city side) head downstream via South Parade and South Quay.

The bridge and quays with attendant shops and houses were designed by John Gwynn, RA and completed in 1792. The fine old brick warehouse buildings have now been converted to flats and a restaurant. The cathedral dominates the way ahead; and beyond the warehouses the view opens up to reveal one of the most elegant spires in the country, 155 feet high, gracefully tapering to the finest of points. It is all that remains of St. Andrew's church and is affectionately known as The Glover's Needle. Along this section of the river a railway ran from about 1860 servicing the warehouses and river trade. It had been intended to link with the canal basin at Diglis but only reached as far as the cathedral. A veritable armada of swans up to 200 strong congregate along this section of the river; when in full flood a handful who have not deserted the city may be seen swimming in the street.

Remain with the riverside with the cathedral looming even larger ahead. When the Watergate, with a house on top, is met turn left into the cathedral precincts.

The Watergate was built in 1378. On its walls are marked flood levels dating back to the seventeenth century. In summer the walkway is well above the normal level of the Severn but even so you have to crane your neck to see the topmost mark - that of 1772 with 1947 coming a close second.

Climbing up from the Watergate swing left through an iron gate. Cross garden areas via old ruins and up steps to the west front of the cathedral. From here there is a fine view upriver to Worcester Bridge and, south-west, to the Malvern Hills. Continue round the building to enter the cathedral by the North Porch.

You will no doubt buy the illustrated guide but it may be useful to highlight a few points of interest - purely a personal selection: the Elgar Memorial Window, a depiction of one of his most famous works, is based on Cardinal Newman's "Dream of Gerontius"; King John's tomb and the choir stalls with their misericords;. Prince Arthur's Chantry chapel (he would have been king instead of Henry VIII but for his early death - the course of history may have been very different) and the nearby window depicting the young prince; the west window and the crypt, a very early part of the cathedral.

Leave by the cloisters but do not, like many visitors, miss the hundreds of small stained glass portraits around all four sides. Here is a colourful kaleidoscope of national and church history: Cuthbert and Lindisfarne; Offa, King of Mercia who once ruled this territory and much of England in the eighth century; Chaucer and Wycliff; Elizabeth I and the Armada; Touching for the Kings Evil - the list is almost endless. Amongst them is the memory of a sad cleric, Thomas Morris, who having refused to swear the oath of allegiance on the accession of William III, lost his living and died a pauper. He directed that he should be remembered by the single word

Miserrimus.

Finally, if time permits choral evensong at the cathedral should delight any music lover.

From the south porch turn left passing the Chapter House of 1120 and leave College Green by the recently restored Edgar Gate. The Kings School occupies various buildings around College Green and the cathedral area. Turn right down Severn Street to visit the Royal Worcester Porcelain Factory, Visitor Centre, Museum and a variety of shops. (Note - it may be necessary to book factory tours in advance.)

Retrace your steps part way and turn right to follow King Street and cross the busy A38/A44 to The Commandery Civil War Centre.

Said to be the city's oldest secular building, this is one of the Worcester museums that should not be missed. Full of interest, it also hosts Civil War encampments and similar events - you may even meet King Charles in person.

After visiting the museum head back towards the city, soon crossing the canal bridge where a plaque commemorates the Battle of Worcester and quotes part of Cromwell's famous letter written late on the night of 3rd September 1651 to the Speaker of the House of Commons: "It is for aught I know a crowning mercy".

Close by was the Sidbury Gate (by the present Kings Head). Built in the thirteenth century and mainly removed in 1768, it was one of six set in the city walls, only a few fragments of which remain. Sidbury Gate and the area around the cathedral was the scene of the bloodiest part of the battle and many died in a last ditch stand to aid the king's escape.

Cross City Walls Road and shortly turn right along Friar Street where a number of timber framed and jettied buildings remain.

Pass The Cardinal's Hat, which claims to be Worcester's oldest pub. The Museum of Local Life is housed in a black and white building of about 1550. Almost opposite, in Union Street, are the Lasletts Alms Houses. Continuing with Friar Street, 26-32 is a long range of timber framed buildings and Grey Friars, on the right, is a splendid jettied house now in the care of the National Trust. Dating from the last quarter of the fifteenth century, Nicholas Pevsner in his famous "Buildings of England" series praises it as one of the finest timber framed buildings in Worcestershire.

From Friar Street continue along New Street, passing the Pheasant Inn, Tudor, with its decorated coaching arch. At the far end of New Street is King Charles House, built in 1577, from which the monarch made his dramatic escape in 1651 - leaving by one door as Cromwell's troops entered the other. This part of the building is now a restaurant with a handsome portrait of the King. Around the corner to the right is a further frontage - now a garden shop - bearing the inscription "Love God - WBS/RD - Honour ye King".

Turn sharp left to follow Mealcheapen Street, cross The Shambles, and ahead on the passage way with the redundant St. Swithun's church to your right.

Pevsner enthuses about the interior. Its treasures include a three-decker pulpit. (Open on Tuesday, Wednesday and Thursday according to circumstances or by application to the tourist information office). Just beyond the iron gates a restaurant now occupies the school founded by Queen Elizabeth in 1561.

Now swing left down the High Street with mostly modern frontages. (Note one of the entrances to the Crown Gate Shopping Centre, Chapel Walk, leads to the restored Countess of Huntingdon chapel, now a popular music centre.)

On the right is the handsome Guildhall of 1721, with a colourfully decorated pediment. Statues of Queen Anne, Charles I and II surround the door above which is the head of Oliver Cromwell with his ears nailed to the wall. Inside there are a number of portraits of local worthies, signed photographs of royalty, items of civic interest and a restaurant in the chandeliered upper storey.

Continue down the High Street. On the right is Fish Street and the County Record Office housed in St. Helen's, the city's mother church. A church has stood here since around 680 although the present building with later restorations is eight centuries younger.

At the foot of the High Street, facing the cathedral and clad in his academic robes, is the statue of Sir Edward Elgar.

I cannot do better than quote from the inscription: "Edward Elgar who rose from obscurity to become England's greatest composer for two hundred years." He was born at Broadheath about 3 miles from the city and later lived in Worcester where his father owned a music shop not far from where his son's statue now stands. "He was organist, violinist, teacher, conductor and self-taught composer. After 1900 his compositions won international recognition, the best known being 'The Dream of Gerontius', the

Cromwell's head - ears nailed to the Guildhall, Worcester

Enigma Variations, the two symphonies, concerto for violin and cello, and 'Land of Hope and Glory'." This last was part of his Pomp and Circumstance marches - who does not know it? After being used in the coronation service of Edward VII in 1902 with words by A.C. Benson, which like Thomas Arne's 'Rule Brittania' written in 1740, struck exactly the right note, it achieved immense and continuing popularity for its stirring patriotic fervour. The inscription continues "He drew his inspiration from the English countryside saying 'Music is in the air all around us'. From 1878 to 1933 he was associated with the Three Choirs Festival, held at Worcester, Hereford & Gloucester". Honours rained down upon Elgar: a knighthood in 1904, Freedom of Worcester in the following year, the Order of Merit 1911, Knight Commander of the Victorian Order

1928, Baronet 1931, Grand Cross of the Victorian Order in 1933. He was further honoured by his appointment as Master of the King's Music 1924 which he held until his death in 1934.

Now our circuit is almost complete, turn right down Deansway. When St. Andrew's spire is reached turn left through gardens to return to the riverside.

7b: Walking out of Worcester - South with The Severn

Starting Point:	Worcester Bridge. Car parking - north of bridge Pitchcroft or Croft Road.	
Distance:	To The Ketch Inn	2¹/₄ miles
	Continuation to Kempsey Church	1³/₄ miles
	Continuation to Severn Stoke	5¹/₂ miles
	Continuation to Upton upon Severn	2³/₄ miles
	Total	12¹/₄ miles
Map:	1.50,000 Landranger 150 Worcester, The Malverns	
	1.25,000 Explorer 204 and 190 (renumbered from 14)	

NOTES: The walks that follow are linear routes on the walk out/bus back principle. Contact numbers for bus services can be found under Useful Information. It should be noted that some services do not operate on Sundays. The sections can of course be walked in instalments. Since this is being written when a Flood Alert has just been issued for the Severn it is appropriate to remind readers that the river can rise very rapidly with extensive flooding possible.

When I lived in London I wrote an article on Walking out of London. The theme was escaping a major city without the use of a car, using public transport to make a return. My suggestion (by no means novel) was to use the canal towpaths. From London it was of course entirely practical to walk all the way to Birmingham if you were so minded, although my walks were designed only for a day out. It's a principle that can be applied to most towns and cities and works particularly well for Worcester. England's second city, as it likes to call itself, is only 30 miles away by towpath using the Worcester & Birmingham Canal, parts of which are explored in earlier chapters.

Having floated the idea I will leave readers to develop their own strategy and take instead to the faster flowing waters of the River Severn.

THE WALK
The Severn Way, southwards, is used for this outing. Since it is signposted from roads, waymarked and also mainly follows the riverbank wayfinding is easy. Several bus services operate from The Ketch Inn on the A38 near the city boundary. Further south longer distance routes, currently 372, 373 and 374 (Midland Red West & Boomerang Bus Company) provide a Mon-Sat hourly service (not evenings) that includes Kempsey, Severn Stoke and Upton. This is only mentioned as a guide - check before you start.

STAGE ONE:
TO THE KETCH INN
From Worcester bridge head south on the east bank of the Severn with South Parade soon becoming a pleasant walkway. The route as far as the cathedral Watergate is described in Walk 7a.

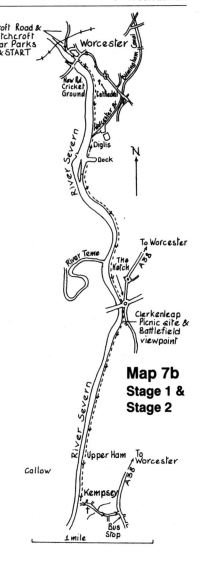

Map 7b
Stage 1 &
Stage 2

From the Watergate continue downstream to Diglis where the Worcester & Birmingham Canal joins the Severn. A signpost indicates river distances on the Severn Navigation, and may encourage walkers as well as river folk: south 16 miles and one lock to Tewkesbury, Gloucester 29 miles and 3 locks, north Stourport 13 miles and 3 locks. Canal cruisers have to work rather harder with 58 locks in the 30 miles to Birmingham.

The Diglis twin locks are soon reached and a further mile will bring you to the Worcester southern bypass bridge. Beyond the bridge take the path which climbs to the Clerkenleap picnic site and the Battle of Worcester viewpoint. An illustrated panel describes the scene as it was at 3pm on the afternoon of 3rd September, 1651. The views extend well beyond the area of conflict and include the Woodbury and Abberley Hills, Shropshire's Clee Hills and the ubiquitous Malverns.

This marks the end of the first stage of the walk. Join the A38 and turn towards the city to find your bus stop by The Ketch Inn to return to the city centre.

STAGE TWO: CONTINUATION TO KEMPSEY

From the Battlefield viewpoint return to the riverside and continue downstream initially under trees. Soon you pass through the Severn Steam Yacht Club grounds with some impressively large boats moored along the riverbank and views to the long dark profile of the Malvern Hills. Beyond the club ground keep with the riverside with Kempsey church seen in the distance. Across the fields to the west will be seen the tower of Powick church still bearing a peppering of scars from the Civil War.

The large low-lying fields benefit from the regular winter flooding as evidenced by the debris left clinging to trees and bushes. Once the flood has receded large lakes are left at both Upper Ham above Kempsey and Lower Ham to the south although the path is clear. Attractive to gulls but not so many wildfowl as might have been expected when I last walked this way.

The handsome building across the river is The Old Manor House at Callow and soon the tower of Stanbrook Abbey will be seen - a Benedictine foundation for nuns.

A bridge is crossed into a caravan site and then the slipway of the Seaborne Yacht Company. At the end of the caravan site cross a stile. If returning by bus turn left to Kempsey church and follow the road to the A38 and the bus stop near The Crown Inn.

STAGE THREE:
KEMPSEY CHURCH TO
SEVERN STOKE

*If joining the walk at Kempsey
church follow Lane's End and
turn left with the Severn Way.
The river is followed as it makes
a large meander round Lower
Ham. Half a mile downstream
from Kempsey the site of the
ancient Pixham Ferry will be
seen with a picnic place on the
opposite bank. It was here that
Simon De Montfort brought
the captive Henry III en route
for the fateful Battle of Evesham
in 1265 in the Barons War.*

*At the end of Lower Ham
cross a stile and continue with
the river until the high bank to
the left crowds in upon you,
then take the signed way up the
slope and over a field to the
white house, Oak Farm. Turn
right with the minor road, Old
Road South, to meet the A38 in
600 yards.*

*Turn right and in 300
yards take the Severn Way
signed on the right.*

As this book is being
compiled I understand that
negotiations are in progress
to bring the next section of
the Severn Way in the
Clifton-Sheepcote Farm
area back to the river sooner
than at present. The existing

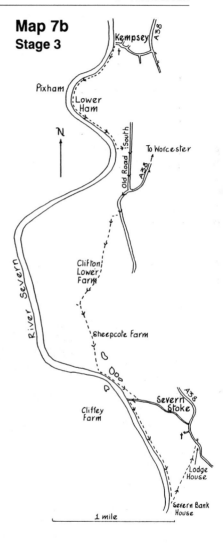

Map 7b
Stage 3

paths which are described here will remain with perhaps some very minor alterations. Watch for the waymarking.

As earlier, the Severn retreating from its incursion into the flood plain leaves behind a legacy of large lagoons. Wildlife was a bit thin in the Kempsey area but here between Clifton and Sheepcote I was well rewarded one January day, first with the sight of ten herons feeding off the wet meadows, then a group of swans enjoying the grazing and calmer waters. Moving on, not less than 500 duck took to the air in a great whirring flight swishing back and forth above my head - an exhilarating sight. Cormorants may also be seen in the trees both summer and winter. These diving fishers, in receipt of much anger from some anglers, are not waterproof and have to retire from the search for food at regular intervals to dry their feathers. Failure to do so could be fatal as they would become waterlogged and drown.

Follow the hedgerow (to your right) for 100 yards then swing left across the field heading roughly in the direction of the house. Continue from the metal gate and on to another stile and continue to stile leaving the house to your left. Bear left along a wire fence. A house lying back from the path has a swan as a thatch bird - very unusual, pheasants are more commonly seen. Maintain your direction to pass Clifton Lower Farm. Here turn left through a gate and right along a hedged track.

When the track comes to an end at a gate and stile go forward with a hedge to your left. This was the fruitful area for the wildfowl. Continue to Sheepcote Farm, cross a farm track and forward on another with a hedge and ditch to your right. In 100 yards cross a stile on the right and swing left over a field soon with a hedge to your left. The path exits to mount the Severn flood bank.

Turn left, downstream soon with the giant gleaming white "tooth" that is the tower of Severn Bank House seen rising above Cliff Wood - a full mile away. In 250 yards the Severn Way is signed off from the river. Once over the stile bear right diagonal with the tower of Severn Stoke church framed between trees. At a lane turn right soon to rejoin the river. (Note - if you turn left with the lane it will bring you to the village in 800 yards if a short cut seems desirable.)

Turn left with the riverbank. The fine brick and timber framed building lying back west of the Severn is Cliffey Farm. Keep with the Severn for the best part of a mile with the Panorama Tower in Croome Park seen on its ridge to your left - a closer view is to be had on Walk 8f. As the riverside path comes to an abrupt end turn left over a stile and follow the grassy track alongside the steep wooded slopes to reach the A38 in half a mile by the Lodge House.

If returning to Worcester by bus turn left to Severn Stoke and the bus stop.

Severn Stoke is a picturesque village. One of its clergy in the seventeenth century had the misfortune to be shot in his pulpit. William Cobbet in his "Rural Rides" mentions a "curiously constructed grape house" owned by a certain Parson St. John at Severn Stoke. I may have missed it and Pevsner does not mention it so perhaps it no longer exists.

STAGE FOUR:
SEVERN STOKE TO
UPTON UPON SEVERN

From the Lodge House at Severn Stoke follow the A38 southwards for 300 yards and then turn right on a No Through Road. In 400 yards beyond a cattle grid the tarmac way divides. Take the left forward fork with the castellated Severn Bank House seen to your right.

As the Coach House is met go forward to a wooden gate and head down the field with Cliff Wood to your right. In 500 yards go through a further gate and ahead to swing left along the Severn for 1¾ miles. Pass under the bridge and back to cross it to enter Upton, an old and attractive town which together with the riverside is described in Walk 8e.

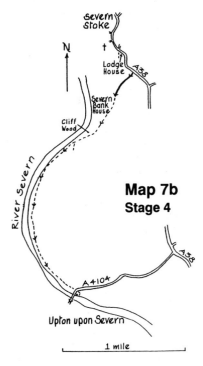

Map 7b
Stage 4

1 mile

7c: *Walking out of Worcester - North with The Severn*

Starting Point: West side Worcester Bridge. Car parking, Tybridge Street (off Hylton Road) on west side. Croft Road or Pitchcroft on city side north of bridge.

Distance:

To Grimley Church	5 miles
Continuation to Holt Fleet	2¹/₄ miles
Continuation to Stourport	6 miles
Total	**13¹/₄ miles**

Map: 1.50,000 Landranger 150 Worcester The Malverns and 138 Kidderminster & Wyre Forest if continuing to Stourport.

1.25,000 Explorer 204 Worcester & Droitwich Spa and for last mile to Stourport Explorer 218 or 219 (Pathfinder 996 Worcester 974 Droitwich and 953 Kidderminster if continuing to Stourport).

NOTES: These are linear walks which can be done in stages with a return by bus although this may not be available on Sundays or in the evenings. At the time of writing several bus services operate along the A443 between Worcester and Holt Heath half a mile west of the Severn at Holt Fleet. One, the 293, continues on the B4196 to Stourport. There is also a service which stops on the east side of the river at Holt Fleet, the 300 Worcester, Hallow, Holt Fleet, Kidderminster Sundays only May-September service and the 304, an hourly Mon/Sat service.

The Severn Way is again brought into play. It follows the west bank of the river northwards from Worcester as far as Grimley then diverts over farmland. At Holt Fleet the route changes to the eastern side. It is waymarked throughout and the small diversions on permissive footpaths around The Camp House and through the quarry near Grimley are particularly well indicated. Walking instructions are therefore minimal. Cormorants, herons, grebes, Canada geese and of course swans may be seen along the way and at The Camp House perhaps something more exotic. Topping all of these was an expected visitor in the summer of 1999. A grey seal spent several weeks in the river far from the sea. It seems to have been following the June salmon run and got at least as far as the Holt Fleet lock some miles above Worcester. Enterprisingly navigating a way through several locks and becoming the envy of fishermen on

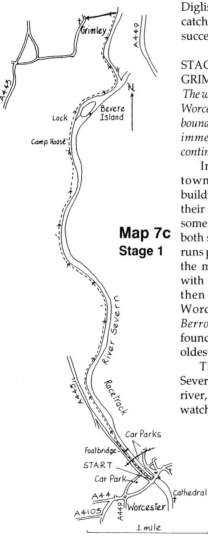

Map 7c
Stage 1

Diglis Weir as they saw the seal catch three large salmon in quick succession

STAGE ONE: WORCESTER TO GRIMLEY

The walk starts from the west side of Worcester bridge with the north bound riverside path joined almost immediately and is followed continuously to Grimley.

Initially there are the townscapes with riverside buildings and steamers admiring their images in the Severn and some fine houses lying back from both sides of the river. The path runs parallel with Hylton Road - the media centre of Worcester with first the BBC studios and then the Evening Mail and Worcester Journal building. *Berrow's Worcester Journal,* founded in 1690, is the world's oldest existing newspaper.

The footbridge over the Severn gives fine views of the river, a good spot from which to watch the Worcester Regatta - a big event which attracts crews from many parts of the country. The bridge also provides a free view of the racecourse that includes the winning post. Racing is said to have been carried on at Pitchcroft

113

for more than 300 years and it was here that the cavalry assembled for the Battle of Worcester in 1651.

The stone that marks the city boundary is reached after about a mile and a half. The west bank houses have fallen back but there are some enviably situated houses on the Barbourne side including the old Ferry House.

A mile from the stone more open country is met as you pass through the G.G.G. Green Park Arboretum and Wild Life Haven. The small plaque on the commemorative seat offers some interesting thoughts on the generosity of God. The long field leads on to The Camp House Inn. (A small diversion here on permissive paths before you are returned to the riverside.) Onward then to Bevere Lock. It was on the island that the bold citizens of Worcester took refuge. Having defied the tax collectors sent by Harthacnut in 1041 the populace wisely had second thoughts and decided that discretion was the better part of valour and retreated before the inevitable retribution arrived. Canada geese may be seen grazing in the fields beneath the small hamlet of Bevere. Soon the tower of Grimley church comes into view. On the east bank the River Salwarpe and the former Droitwich Canal join the Severn.

Keep with the riverside until a footbridge brings you to a rough lane. Here turn left to reach the village of Grimley in a quarter of a mile. Turn left soon passing the Wagon Wheel and continue to the church.

There are two diverse literary connections at Grimley. Mrs. Henry Wood (née Price), the author of "East Lynne", was the granddaughter of a Grimley resident whose fortunes derived from the gloving industry. Lucien Bonaparte, brother of Napoleon, having been taken prisoner spent many years in relaxed captivity at Thorngrove occupying his time in writing poetry.

STAGE TWO: GRIMLEY TO HOLT FLEET

Take the signed path through the churchyard and turn left along a field edge and then right (ignore path waymarked left) to reach a stile from which you look forward to Church Farm Quarry. There are some permissive routes here which may change according to the development of the quarry. Descend towards a waymarked power line and forward to steps over the conveyor belts and into the quarry area. Here large blue arrows direct walkers. There is much activity with large dumper trucks and the like.

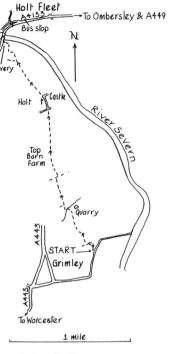

Map 7c
Stage 2

Currently the way through curves to the right then bears left to cross a stream beyond a large pool. Turn left with a strip of woodland to meet a stile by a quarry access road. Turn right and in a few yards forward through a gate on the bridleway that leads towards Top Barn Farm.

As you reach a T junction of tracks turn right and then shortly left climbing to Top Barn. Follow the waymarked route through the small industrial unit estate to metal gate and bridleway which leads to the hamlet of Holt via open fields; giving some of the best views of the day which include the Woodberry and Abberley Hills. Continue with
the surfaced road between the church and Holt Castle.

Holt Castle, a private residence, is on a site said to have been occupied for a thousand years. The fourteenth century tower was built by John Beauchamp (1319-1388) later to become Baron Kidderminster. John had an adventurous career in a time when politics were even tougher than they are today. In 1340 he took part in the Battle of Sluys, the big naval engagement of the Hundred Years War with the French. Six years later, he was with Edward III at the Battle of Crecy when despite being outnumbered the English, thanks to the superior fire power of the archers and good generalship, inflicted a major defeat on the French. John Beauchamp was Member of Parliament for Worcester for periods between 1352 and 1380 and knighted in 1385. Later he was appointed Justice of North Wales

115

during Richard II's reign. But the tide of favour was turning for John Beauchamp and others. The Lords Appellant in the course of their campaign to restrict the monarch's power brought charges of treason against several of Richard's supporters, John Beauchamp amongst them and he was executed at Tower Hill.

The Bromley family later owned Holt Castle. Thomas Bromley (1530-1587) became a lawyer, was Solicitor General in 1569 and led the prosecution of the Duke of Norfolk for treason in 1572. In 1586 he was appointed by Elizabeth I as judge for the trial of Mary Queen of Scots which led to her eventual execution.

Sir Henry Bromley became implicated in Robert Devereaux, the Earl of Essex's ill fated revolt against Elizabeth I. Essex died under the axe. Bromley after imprisonment in the tower was released by James I and later as High Sheriff of Worcester was involved in the arrest of the Gunpowder plotters.

Another Henry Bromley owned the castle during the Civil War and being on the King's side was fined £4000 for his allegiance to the Crown when hostilities ended (for a time) in 1646.

A quarter of a mile from Holt church, as the road bends left, join a footpath on the right bearing half right to descend to a stile and forward through a wooded area to decant into the car park of the Holt Fleet Carvery. Turn right to cross the bridge to find your bus stop opposite the Wharf Inn.

STAGE THREE: HOLT FLEET TO STOURPORT

From the east side of the bridge descend to the riverbank and head upstream. The first section of this walk is described in Chapter 5d, p78. When the route turns inland continue with the Severn - there is a continuous right of way to Stourport.

8
Malvern - Hills, Commons and The Severn Plain

The hills that loom protectively over Malvern and its eponymous neighbours are composed in part of some of the oldest rock in Britain, formed 900 million years ago. Houses rise up the lower slopes but are eventually obliged to give up the unequal struggle. They were built to picturesque effect, imparting a continental flavour to this very English former spa town.

The growth of the spa town was as much social as the advertised medical benefits. At least that is how they appear to have developed. Indeed the somewhat harsh regimes of some "water cures" suggest the need for physical fitness before they were undertaken if the patient was to survive the more rigorous treatments. Faith in the healing qualities of the water predate the creation of Malvern as a spa town. A spring a little above the present Holy Well was held to be a valuable treatment for diseases of the eye in Elizabethan times. Malvern joined in the prosperity of the eighteenth century "spa fever", with the famous Dr. John Wall amongst the founders. Dr. Wall it will be remembered was something of an entrepreneur for he was also the moving spirit in the setting up of the Worcester, (now Royal) Porcelain factory.

Malvern water, filtered through the age old rocks, has a reputation for purity. Those sampling it for the first time are apt to be disappointed for the keenest palate will find it bland to the point of having no taste whatsoever. Malvern water is commercially bottled, finding a place on many a supermarket shelf, but can be sampled without charge at several points around the hills. A fashionable meeting place for those taking the cure was St. Ann's Well. To reach it climb the 99 steps from the centre of Malvern and continue on the steep winding way to the octagonal building that still provides refreshments. Water trickles from the wellhead in the adjoining building, with a poetic paean on a tablet on the wall.

Two miles down the A449 a minor road leads to Holy Well

117

covered by the well-house of 1843 and restored a few years ago -
here again the water may be tasted. There are also spouts channelling
water directly from the hills. The one that attracts most attention is
on the B4232, the West Malvern Road. This is often a busy spot with
a small queue of people filling bottles - some apparently having
travelled considerable distances to replenish their supplies.

Malvern's spa buildings are now following other careers but the
Winter Gardens Theatre continues into its second century, refreshed
with a lotte. y grant. Many famous names have been associated with
the Malvern Festival, among them Sir Barry Jackson, founder of the
Birmingham Repertory Theatre, director of the Royal Shakespeare
Theatre at Stratford and London's Covent Garden Opera. Sir Edward
Elgar lived locally and was involved as was the distinguished Irish
wit, theatre critic and playwright George Bernard Shaw. The
internationally acclaimed singer Jenny Lind spent her retirement at
Wynds Point; busts of the "Swedish Nightingale", and "England's
greatest composer for 200 years", Elgar, will be found in the park by
the Winter Gardens. Sir Edward not only enjoyed his walks on the
hills but found inspiration there, as did the fourteenth century
clergyman and poet William Langland who was educated in
Malvern's Benedictine monastery. It is said that tiring from a long
walk on the hills he paused to rest and fell asleep. His dreams led to
his writing the famous allegorical social and religious commentary
"The Vision of Piers the Plowman". A copy in the language of the
day may be seen in the Abbey Gate museum in Malvern.

Malvern's oldest and most imposing building is its Priory
church, founded in 1095, but with later restorations. Misericords,
medieval tiles and fine stained glass are features of the church.
Viewed from the hills it stands head and shoulders above the town.
The tall tower which is almost all that remains of Little Malvern
Priory is viewed to similar, even more dramatic, effect from the
eastern ramparts of the British Camp.

End to end the hills run for a little under 9 miles but the switch-
backing traverse from the south from Chase End's 627 feet summit
via Ragged Stone and Midsummer Hills to the British Camp and
onward to the Worcestershire Beacon (1394 feet) thence over North
Hill and End Hill, is rather more than the flat map measurement. To
use a modern phrase the Malvern Hills are user friendly with many

Malvern Water for free from a spout on the West Malvern Road

car parks from which to take long or short walks, along the crest or the many paths that terrace the slopes on either side. The routes that follow provide an introduction and perhaps inspiration for further outings. Meanwhile some popular approaches to the main points are given below.

The easiest route to the Worcestershire Beacon is from the Beacon Road Car Park, just off the West Malvern Road by the Wyche Crossing. From here the path leads to the summit in three-quarters of a mile. A less direct and more strenuous route starts from Malvern's Rosebank Gardens via the 99 steps. The Herefordshire Beacon, otherwise the British Camp, is probably the most visited viewpoint and can be reached aided by a stepped path, from the large car park by the Malvern Hills Hotel. This is located on the A449, 3¹/₂ miles south of Great Malvern. The Hollybush Pass provides a launching point for walks northwards to Midsummer Hill and south to Raggedstone and Chase End Hills.

Throughout the views are superb and wide ranging. Southwards into Gloucestershire with the tree crowned May Hill at Newent is prominent. Westwards is the rolling countryside of Herefordshire into Wales, with the distinctive cone of the Sugar Loaf near Abergavenny easily picked out. The long line of the Black Mountains' Hatterrall Ridge rises like a great wall and, on a good day, the Brecon Beacons themselves may be seen. The hills of Shropshire include Titterstone Clee and, nearer at hand, Worcestershire's Woodberry and Abberley Hills. To the east the slopes fall to the commons, which provide further good walking and the villages of the Severn valley. Onwards to Bredon Hill with the Cotswold escarpment making the final backdrop.

The hillforts on Midsummer Hill and the Herefordshire Beacon have been mentioned but other landmarks include a glimpse of Eastnor Castle, built in 1812, and the tall finger to the sky which is the commemorative obelisk to the Somers family. The view up the hills from the British Camp over Wynds Point is the best known but perhaps the most appealing is that from the eastern ramparts or Broad Down which includes the British Camp Reservoir - the little blue eye of the hills. The Malvern Hills have their own mythology. Clutters Cave is said to have sheltered a giant of uncertain temper who hurled a stone at a man seen speaking to his wife in the village of Colwall - quite a feat and no one has yet found it prudent to move it from where it fell.

A hands and knees crawl up the stony slopes of Ragged Stone Hill was one of the punishments meted out to the monks of Little Malvern who had offended in some way. One in his agony is said to have placed a curse on "all those upon whom the shadow of the hill shall fall". A great trough was dug along the crest of the range in 1290 - the Red Earl's Ditch. Its purpose was to resolve a long running dispute by marking out the boundary between the lands held by Gilbert de Clare, the Earl of Gloucester and those of the Bishop of Hereford. As the Shire Ditch it continues to define the county boundary. Also surviving is the legend that it was artfully designed so that deer having jumped into the Earl's side could not return to the Lord Bishop's territory. Just beyond the Beacon Road car park is the site of a gold mine. A Bristol prospector, William Williams, spent ten years and all his money digging deep into the hills in an unproductive quest for the yellow metal. The only gold that can be guaranteed today is in the spectacular colour that clothes the hills in autumn.

8a: The Worcestershire Beacon

Starting Point:	Car park off the North Malvern Road (B4232) close to the Clock Tower.
Distance:	5¾ or 5 miles
Map:	1.50,000 Landranger 150 Worcester & the Malverns
	1.25,000 Explorer 190 (renumbered from 14) Malvern Hills and Bredon Hill

NOTES: This walk explores the northern end of the Malvern Hills, with an initially strenuous start but the effort will be amply rewarded by the extensive views on offer.

THE WORCESTERSHIRE BEACON is "Malvern's lonely height" of Lord Macaulay's poem "The Armada". This described in graphic detail the spread of "the fiery herald" as beacons were lit across the nation to warn of the approach of the Spanish Armada in 1588. It begins, if I remember rightly, "Night sank upon the dusky beach and on the purple sea, Such a night in England ne'er had been, nor ere again shall be". It was an especially popular poem during the 1940s with a parallel with the sirens that were nightly sounded to send the population to the air raid shelters.

Views to all points of the compass are on offer - the toposcope on the 1394 foot summit will assist in picking out hills both near and far. As a bonus there is the opportunity to sample the famous Malvern water - and for free!

There is a multiplicity of paths but the way over the Beacon and on to the Gold Mine is straightforward. Remember that in the event of any confusion from this point, your general line of travel is north. From St. Ann's Well the route is again fairly easy to follow.

THE WALK

From the car park retrace your steps to the road. Turn left and immediately beyond the clock tower take the path on the left signed North Hill, Table Hill and Sugar Loaf. (The clock tower was built in 1901 "in the first year of the reign of his most gracious majesty King Edward VII".)

A long climb, at first aided by a stepped path, leads through the former North Malvern Quarry and on between the hills. Ignore all left and right turns and continue beyond a large and solitary tree to cross a broad track by a wooden seat. A glance back presents a widening view with the bracken and grass covered slopes of End Hill in the foreground backed by the red tiled roofs and white walled houses of North Malvern and the distant Abberley Hills.

Follow the path between North Hill and Table Hill to the top of the

Map 8a

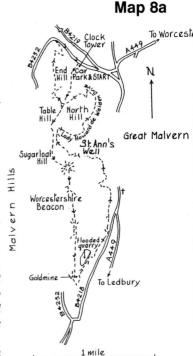

122

rise to reveal the majestic north face of the Worcestershire Beacon. The way divides - go half right descending to a junction of paths to continue over the intermediate height of the Sugar Loaf. Here you may look westwards over the Herefordshire countryside and on to the mountains of Wales. Another Sugar Loaf is to be seen, a volcanic cone 30 miles distant, and the 11 mile long high wall of the Black Mountains culminating in the sharp fall from Hay Bluff. The Shropshire Hills have been added to the northern arc, Brown Clee and Titterstone Clee - this last topped by the white golf ball of an earth satellite station which may be seen glinting in the sun. Eastwards lies the Severn Plain and beyond Bredon Hill, waiting to be enjoyed on another day.

Descend, slight left from the Sugar Loaf making for the round marker stone that points to paths in all directions. Take any of the paths that climb to the summit of the Beacon to enjoy the even wider views from the toposcope, which now includes the Cotswolds escarpment in the east and in the west if it is a clear day, the Brecon Beacons - 50 miles away.

From the Beacon descend southwards with the man-made contours of the British Camp prominent, the Somers obelisk and, more distantly the tree crowned May Hill near Newent. The tarmac emergency access road should be ignored in favour of the green tracks. (This metalled way to the summit is an essential feature - fierce fires are a frequent occurrence in a dry summer.) Continue past a covered reservoir to a further marker stone. This is the site of the gold mine mentioned in the last chapter. Here turn sharp left signed Quarry Walk and St. Ann's Well via Earnslaw. Ignore the first right fork, and when the path divides again keep forward descending through woodland to the foot of the quarry. A small diversion reveals the quarry face and the pool below.

From the quarry go forward, slight right on a good track which falls almost to the road before rising again. Remain with the main track which parallels the road. At the top of a rise by a clump of trees there is a good view to Great Malvern and its Priory Church. The path veers left as it rounds a cleft in the hillside before continuing northwards to St. Ann's Well.

A cafe at the Well House provides refreshments (opening varies according to the season) and a verse by the well-head invites you to "Drink from this crystal fountain...". Continue with the now rising path with St. Ann's Well to your right and shortly bear left on the track that runs above Green Valley.

Curve right under the Sugar Loaf making towards North Hill. In 200 yards bear right on a wide track - this is Lady Howard de Walden Drive. Ignore the grassy path to the summit. Remain with the drive as it terraces the upper slopes of North Hill. There are views down to Malvern with Worcester coming into view in the north-east.

Ignore the tracks that run off to the right. As you round North Hill, Table Hill comes into view and the path reaches the seat passed on your outward journey. You may turn right here to retrace your way back to the car park.

Alternatively continue with the track for a short way then descend before climbing to the summit of End Hill. Continue with another dip and rise before falling steeply to turn right on a broad track. This winds down to meet the West Malvern Road at a sharp bend - care needed. Turn right and take the road back to the clock tower and your starting point.

8b: Broad Down, Midsummer Hill and the Herefordshire Beacon

Starting Point:	Wynds Point car park, opposite the Malvern Hills Hotel, A449, 4 miles south of Great Malvern
Distance:	7 miles
Map:	1.50,000 Landranger 150 Worcester, The Malverns
	1.25,000 Explorer 190 (was 14) Malvern Hills and Bredon Hill.

NOTES: This walk crosses part of the commons that lie under the eastern slopes of the Malvern Hills. Water leaching out of the hillside may make it a little squidgy underfoot in places. Definitely a boot walk.

THE HILLFORTS

This circuit concludes with the spectacular prospect from the northern ramparts of the British Camp on the Herefordshire Beacon, which is so often reproduced as the archetypal view of the Malvern Hills. The Iron Age fort, added to over many generations, is said to be amongst the finest in Britain. Banks and ditches cut into the steep slopes protect the central area within which were the residential huts. A very rough measurement gives a north-south length of 900 yards and about 300 yards across. By AD48 the Romans in the process of securing their frontiers evicted the residents of both the

The British Camp, otherwise known as the Herefordshire Beacon

British Camp and that on Midsummer Hill a mile to the south. Estimates of the population of the British Camp range up to 1500 or more. It is included in rather a long list of places reputed to be where Caractacus fought his last courageous battle against the Roman invaders. Eleven hundred years later the Normans, conscious of the strategic worth of the site, added the castle mound which now forms the highest point of the fort. No definite date seems to have been attributed to the building of the first fort here. Midsummer Hill, only a little smaller in area, had up to 250 huts within the ramparts and seems to have been in use from about 400BC, until it was torched by the Romans. The man with overall responsibility for these military operations was the Governor of Britain, Ostorius Scapula. He was a man with many problems on his hands and a reputation at stake for the warlike British were making incursions into Roman-held territory and Wales was yet to be subdued.

THE WALK
Three paths head southwards from the car park - take the middle one signed

Pink Cottage. This climbs steadily, soon beneath the ramparts of the British Camp and above the oval shaped reservoir and beyond to a widening view of the Cotswolds and Bredon Hill.

When a round marker stone is met, about half a mile from the car park, turn left over Broad Down. This is another good point to take in the view, the carefully engineered fortifications of the British Camp and the succession of peaks running northwards to the Worcestershire Beacon. Do not continue to the end of the path at the edge of Broad Down which overlooks the reservoir but take the path seen on the right through grass and bracken to descend through woodland.

Keep ahead as you emerge into the open to join a rough track, passing Dales Hall. Leave the track when it swings left and go forward over the open common under Swinyard Hill to meet a minor road. Turn left to reach a house called Berrow Down - just opposite a small willow fringed pond.

Here leave the road turning right on a path that at first runs near to the right-hand boundary. Do not be tempted onto the path which runs off diagonally left. Continue, passing Bradford Farm and Tyrus House to cross Hollybed Common. When a track is met bear right with it to pass the Mill Pond on your left - about three-quarters of a mile from Berrow Down.

Follow the rising path to join the road (A438) by a small car park. Turn right to reach the top of the Hollybush Pass in about half a mile. A little after passing quarry gates take the broad track on the right (informal car parking here) and swing up the grassy hillside, then under trees to the fort on Midsummer

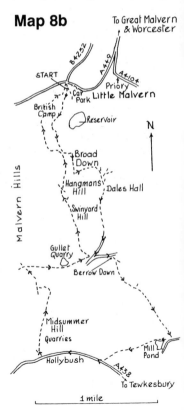

Map 8b

Hill (National Trust and about 940 feet high).

At the northern end of the fort swing left on a curving path which falls to meet a lane. Turn right, passing Midsummer Cottage and, in 200 yards, right on a track through woodland to the high cliff and deep pool of Gullet Quarry. Follow the path round the edge of the pool and past a cottage to reach a car park at the edge of the common. Take the stony track on the left, a long steady climb along Swinyard Hill, passing Foxhall and a view to Pink Cottage tucked under the slopes of Hangmans Hill.

Ignore two right turns, one signed Castlemorton, to meet a further junction. Continue forward, signed Giant's Cave and British Camp. Soon after emerging into more open ground the promised cave is passed on your right - a modest shelter cut into the rock face. Its use is a matter of speculation - is it where the giant lived, or a hermit, a shelter for a lookout or the start of a mine in which interest was quickly lost? Continue to the marker stone by Broad Down and bear left on the steep path to the British Camp. Far below is the reservoir and beyond the tower of Little Malvern Priory. When well up the hillside there is a choice of routes: follow the eastern or western ramparts or make your way through the centre to the Norman castle mound.

The northern end of the fort provides the superb view northwards over Wynds Point and on to Pinnacle Hill and the Worcestershire Beacon - the most photographed scene on the Malvern Hills that has graced many a calendar.

Descend by the stepped path to return to the car park.

8c: *Common Ground*

Starting Point:	Car park on the common - B4208 on the south-western edge of Welland. Welland is on the A4104; 4 miles west of Upton upon Severn.
Distance:	7 miles
Map:	1.50,000 Landranger 150 Worcester, The Malverns
	1.25,000 Explorer 190 (was14) Malvern Hills, Bredon Hill

NOTES: Motorists watch out for livestock which may wander on to the roads.

Quiet lanes connect the three commons featured in this walk - Shadybank, Hollybed and Castlemorton - which offer superb views to the Malvern Hills, at their most colourful in autumn. More magic

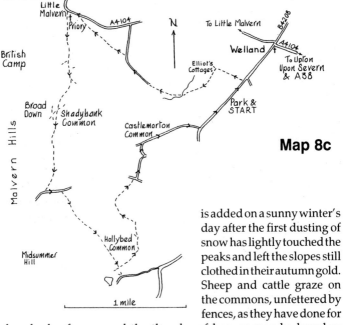

is added on a sunny winter's day after the first dusting of snow has lightly touched the peaks and left the slopes still clothed in their autumn gold. Sheep and cattle graze on the commons, unfettered by fences, as they have done for hundreds of years and the thunder of hooves may be heard as ponies and their young riders enjoy a brisk gallop.

There is room for all to enjoy the spacious commons throughout the year with easy walking on good tracks, but parts can be soggy in winter and after rain.

THE WALK

From the car park area retrace your steps to the 40 mph and Welland village signs. Turn left on the grassy track heading towards the hills. Views open out to the full 9 mile run of the range with the tall tower of Little Malvern Priory seen ahead as you advance to Marlbank Farm.

Bear left as the farm gate is reached, passing Elliot's Cottages, and beyond the next house bear right on a metalled track. Turn right as it crosses the Marlbank Brook and then left beyond the bridge. Continue past Cider Mill Cottage with millstones at its wall, to reach the gated Hancock Lane.

Walkers heading for the Worcestershire Beacon
Little Malvern Priory from the British Camp

Remain with the lane until about 100 yards after it curves to the right. Take the signed track on the left which runs between trees towards Millbrook Cottage which is passed on your left. Shortly a stile leads into an open field with further views to the hills.

Head over the fields in the general direction of Little Malvern Priory guided by waymarked stiles to reach the road, the A4104. Turn left to pass or visit the church.

While still ministering to the local community only the tower and an attenuated church remains of the Benedictine foundation of 1171, dissolved in 1536 under Henry VIII's reforms that saw so many similar monasteries swept away - the good, the bad and the indifferent. Not all the treasures found their way into Henry's coffers - some items were legitimately acquired from the King's commissioners. Much was not, for like a ship thrown up on the beach after a great storm it was often a free for all with lead stripped from roofs and the stonework a ready-made quarry. Some of the houses of Pershore are said to have been built at least in part from materials removed from the town's abbey - once amongst the greatest in Britain.

A little beyond the Priory turn left on the bridleway that edges Little Malvern Court with stolen glimpses of its well-sculptured topiary and water gardens. As height is gained there is a view over the commons to Bredon Hill and the Cotswold escarpment. Continue beyond the timber framed Underhill Farm to a gate where the track divides. Go forward rising along the hedge line to meet a gate. Continue with the track as it crosses Shadybank Common, merging with other paths to pass Dales Hall and Broomhill Coppice to your left.

As the trees fall back leave the track and go forward over the common to reach the road. Turn left and immediately after passing the house called Berrow Down turn right on an indistinct path, with at first the hedge line to your right. Maintain your general direction passing Bradford Farm to cross Hollybed Common with its network of tracks (not all of which appear upon maps).

Make towards the white houses seen ahead but 100 yards before they are reached swing left on a grassy track. There is another good view from here to the crest and troughs of the hills as they roll northwards to the

---

Broadway Tower

Worcestershire Beacon.

Make towards the houses of Hollybed Street, aiming for the end house in the row and here bear left following a rough track along a hedgerow. At The Myttons swing left to follow the boundary of the common with an improving track. Turn right on a quiet lane passing a house called Huntsbridge and then Paddocks with a fine dovecote.

At a junction of lanes turn right then almost immediately left. Bear right with the lane as a pond is seen to your left and curving left as you pass Eight Oaks Farm. At the top of a rise turn right at a junction, following the edge of Castlemorton Common to meet the B4208. Turn left. This is a busy road but grassy paths alongside the common may be followed to return you to your starting point.

8d: Kempsey Common and Pirton

Starting Point:	Kempsey Common car park. Kempsey is on the A38, 3¹/₂ miles south of Worcester then take Bestmans Lane signed Napleton and Kempsey Common for 1 mile with car park located by the Farmers Arms.
Distance:	6¹/₄ miles
Map:	1.50,000 Landranger 150 Worcester, The Malverns
	1.25,000 Explorer 190 (was 14) Malvern Hills and Bredon Hill.

NOTES: Gentle slopes offer wide ranging views from modest heights. Families may like to note in advance that the main railway track has to be crossed at Narrow Wood.

KEMPSEY

Simon de Montfort, Earl of Leicester, came this way in 1265. The second phase of the Barons War was coming to a head and he was on his way to join up with desperately needed reinforcements led by his son. Alas the young De Montfort had dallied with side issues on the way to answer his father's summons. Further, he had suffered from a surprise night attack at Kenilworth which had thrown his forces into disarray and led to his late arrival at Evesham.

The Earl had crossed the river by the Pixham Ferry and stayed the night in the Kempsey Manor of the Bishop of Worcester, Walter de Cantelupe. The bishop said mass before his guest retired. It is tempting to speculate that perhaps the bishop had some premonition - certainly it proved to be the Earl's last night in a soft bed. Within 36 hours he was being laid to his eternal rest beneath the high altar of Evesham Abbey.

De Montfort was the power behind the throne. Henry III was a spent man, not so his son Edward, who had escaped from imprisonment in Hereford. The future Edward I, aided by the Earl of Gloucester who had changed his allegiance, and cavalry under Roger Mortimer, emerged the victor of Evesham. The Earl, who had initiated the first moves to a parliamentary democracy, was outnumbered, outmanoeuvred and outwitted. He went into battle, a brave man who knew full well his fate. "Let us commend our souls to God" he said, when the full realisation of his situation dawned upon him, "...for our bodies are theirs".

THE WALK

From the car park head to the top left corner of the green area - ignore the first path which is signed through a metal gate. In a few yards bear left, briefly near the hedge then take a diagonal course up the slope leaving the white painted Common Farm well to your left.

There are views, north-westerly, to the Abberley and Woodberry Hills with the Big Ben style clock tower set between them. The red

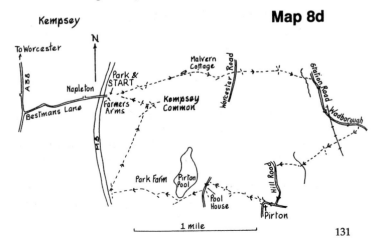

Map 8d

roofs of Worcester, the cathedral tower and the elegant spire of St. Andrew's all contribute to the scene. As you reach the crest of the ridge, turn and look back. The full length of the Malvern Hills runs along the western horizon, a fine prospect that will be repeated from several points of the walk.

Your passage over the short cropped grass will bring you to the boundary, which is followed to pass a group of white buildings. Continue to the brick house seen ahead, Malvern Cottage, with Bredon Hill now seen away to your right. Follow the broad track to pass Stonehall Farm and a pool to your left. Head at a slight left angle to the top corner of the common and exit by a metal gate.

Here the path divides. Keep ahead on a narrow way between brambles and gorse to meet Worcester Road, not the broad highway the name suggests but a quiet lane. Cross and keep ahead on a signed bridleway to meet a metal gate. There is a view here over the gently rolling landscape towards Pershore.

Head directly down the slope of the very large field - the pasture may still be divided by electric fencing. The walker's way is eased by insulated spring-loaded hooks that avoid that nervous step over or under the wire.

Bredon Hill, to your right, is now much more prominent - a local weather guide if an old rhyme is to be believed - "When Bredon Hill puts on its hat, Men of the Vale, beware of that". Beyond Bredon are more hills - the smoky grey blur of the Cotswolds merging into the distance.

At the foot of the field go forward, with a fence to your right, over a waymarked footbridge and on to meet and turn right on to a lane towards Wadborough via a level crossing. A quarter of a mile from the crossing, opposite a clump of willow trees, turn right through a short section of Narrow Wood. Bear right to follow the outside edge of the wood and at the bottom of the field into the wood to meet and cross the railway tracks.

CAUTION - THIS IS THE MAIN LINE EXPRESS ROUTE.

Go orward, with a hedge to your right. At the end of a second field cross a stream, bear right and go up the hill to meet Hill Road. Turn left and in 500 yards, right, signed Croome, High Green and Pershore. In 200 yards bear left to visit St. Peter's church, Pirton.

St. Peter's church, which looks out over its scattered parish, is rather special having a rare timber framed tower - 500 to 600 years old - topped by a steep pitched, tiled, candle snuffer roof. The notice board gives details of where the key can be obtained in the event of the church being locked. A unique item came to light here in 1871, the Pirton Stone, too precious to be left unguarded in a country church and now in Oxford's Ashmolean Museum. Only a few inches in size the embossed stone depicts a decorated cross and is thought to have been used as a stamp or mould for making badges for pilgrims.

From the church retrace your steps a short distance to the bend in the road. Take the path on the left beyond a metal gate and downhill on a broad track. Go forward with a hedge to your right over the next two fields, at the end of which a narrow tread may be seen going directly ahead - this does not appear to be a right of way although it does lead to the road. Here is one of those dilemmas walkers in arable country sometimes meet. The OS map shows a path heading at an angle to the top left corner of a large field making towards Pool House; indeed it is thus signed from the road at Pool House. When I was last there the field was under crop, no path or boot tread visible. It seems possible that the way forward along the hedgerow may be used although technically this could be regarded as trespass. Turn left at the road and just beyond Pool House take the path on the right, signed Kerswell Green, through a short piece of woodland to a gate with a request from the Croome Estate to keep to the paths with dogs on lead.

Head slight diagonally left over gently rising old parkland, to the southern end of Pirton Pool, with its wildfowl including swans and Canada geese. From the tip of the pool head up the slope to the northern end of the woodland seen ahead. From the crest of the rise descend to a waymarked gate and forward climbing to pass a clump of trees to your left. Another fine view to the Malvern Hills from here. Descend with Park Farm to your right to exit by the waymarked stile and keep forward with a hedgerow on your right and the roar of the motorway growing louder at every step.

Turn right at the foot of the field, through a metal gateway and in a short distance head half right up the hillside towards a strip of woodland. Go through a metal gate and forward with woodland and a fence on your left. In 700 yards, near the top of the slope (triangulation point seen a little ahead), cross the stile on your left and bear right on a narrow tread which edges towards the left-hand hedgerow. Soon turn left on a broad grassy track descending to your starting point with further views to Worcester along the way.

8e: Upton upon Severn

Starting Point: Free car park by sports field, opposite church at southern end of the town - A4104.

Distance: 4 miles

Map: 1.50,000 Landranger 150 Worcester, The Malverns

1.25,000 Explorer 190 (was 14) Malvern Hills and Bredon Hill.

NOTES: Level walking - grazing land.

UPTON UPON SEVERN is a pleasant, much visited riverside town a few miles downstream from Worcester with buildings a mix of Georgian brick and earlier timber framed houses. It is a town well used to receiving visitors and is a popular mooring point for waterway cruisers who may be following the Avon, Severn and Birmingham canals ring. It also hosts an annual and growing jazz festival.

For hundreds of years the Welsh drovers came this way, via Hereford, Ledbury and over the Malvern Hills, thence on to Broadway to link with the route from Worcester.

The town's inns did a good trade and not only from thirsty drovers. Upton was an important river port, with a wooden bridge replaced by stone towards the end of the sixteenth century. Local tax payers rebelled at having to contribute to the cost and it took an act of parliament to ensure its completion. It is said that in 1705 the stone from the tower, all that remained of Hanbury castle, was plundered to effect urgently needed repairs.

The quayside would have been buzzing with activity, with hundreds of barges doing a two way traffic in all manner of goods. Long trains of packhorses transported goods far inland, both eastwards and west into Wales. It is with good reason that one of the local inns which dates from 1601 is called the Olde Anchor Inn. The White Lion found its way into the pages of fiction in Henry Fielding's *Tom Jones* published in 1749. It was, according to the book "…a house of exceedingly good repute". The inn according to the book was also the scene of a considerable disturbance which is alluded to in The Torrington Diaries as "The Second Battle of Upton."

The town's main landmark is the former thirteenth century church of which only the tower remains. A cupola added in 1780 gave it a certain distinction and is affectionately referred to as The Pepperpot.

Opposite the Pepperpot is the Tudor House and Cromwell's Chocolates - a rather special confectioners, with more than a local trade. It was here on the 29th August 1651 that Oliver Cromwell was met with "...an abundance of joy and extraordinary shouting after the decisive battle of Upton".

Being between Royalist Worcester and Roundhead Gloucester the town was inevitably and unenviably involved in the Civil War; particularly with the arrival in Worcester in August 1651, hotfoot from Scotland, of Charles II in pursuit of his father's lost crown. The Royalists established outposts to guard the important river crossings of the Teme at Powick and the Severn at Upton. In charge at Upton was a Colonel Massey, the Parliamentarian governor of Gloucester who had so successfully withstood the Royalist siege of that city a few years earlier. Now a change of heart had placed him on the king's side.

A contingent of cavalry was based at Hanbury Castle - no doubt to the distress of its owner Sir Nicholas Lechmere who was of the Parliamentary persuasion and had taken part in the siege and subsequent surrender of Worcester in 1646. To shorten a long story to the bare essentials, a guard had been placed on Upton Bridge from which all but one plank had been removed. Poor military discipline left the bridge unguarded for the vital moments when a small reconnoitring party from Cromwell's army slipped across the river at dawn. Their presence was soon spotted and the alarm raised. Cromwell's men took refuge in the church and held out despite a fierce attack and efforts to burn down the building. Reinforcements arrived and by nightfall the town was in Parliamentarian hands. A small battle which was turned to good effect in the following days that led to the final onslaught on Worcester and the desperate flight of the king.

One of the town's strangest inhabitants was John Dee (1527-1608), appointed Rector of Upton upon Severn in 1557. He was a brilliant mathematician who tutored royalty but whose other activities were tinged with mystery, magic and the macabre. He became a friend of the famous map-maker, Mercator, and gained some repute as a conjuror which was later to lead him to darker things. He successfully defended himself in the face of accusations of attempting to poison Queen Mary. His skill as an astrologer was such that he was commissioned to select a day of suitable auguries for the coronation of Queen Elizabeth and he continued as her adviser. He purported to own a "magic crystal" and became deeply involved in the study of alchemy. Dee claimed to be able to converse both with angels and evil spirits and was associated with a much

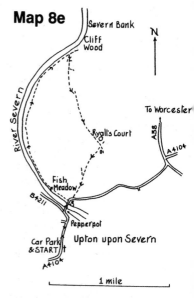

Map 8e

Severn Bank
Cliff Wood
N
River Severn
To Worcester
Ryall's Court
A38
A4104
Fish Meadow
B4211
Pepperpot
Car Park & START
Upton upon Severn
A4104
1 mile

younger man Edward Kelly (a.k.a. Talbot) with similar "talents" of necromancy and the conversion of base metal to gold. Apparently Dee was unaware of Kelly's convictions for forgery - as a result of which he had lost both ears. He disguised this disfigurement by the permanent wearing of a black skull cap. How much Dee was taken in is a matter of speculation - could a man of much learning be so naive?

In the old churchyard by the Pepperpot is a bust of Admiral Sir William Tennant, KCB, CVE, MVO who was the senior naval officer at the evacuation of the British Army from Dunkirk in 1940.

THE WALK

From the car park turn left down Old Street and continue into the High Street enjoying the architecture of the town and the individuality of the shops and inns. Lloyds bank, for example, is housed in a bow-fronted building which would equally do well as an antique shop. Pass the Old Anchor Inn of 1601, a reminder of Upton's past history as a busy river port.

136

The Pepperpot, Upton upon Severn

Beyond the Kings Head, with its pack of cards inn sign, join the riverside, bear left to pass The Plough and cross the bridge over the Severn.

Now turn right signed Severn Way and swing left under the road, signed Public Bridleway Severn Stoke, and into Fish Meadow. From here the river is followed without the need for further directions for about 1¾ miles.

The village of Hanley Castle is seen on the opposite bank - the castle built by King John in 1210 has long gone save the moat. The castle was given by Henry III to Gilbert de Clare - the man responsible for the construction of the shire ditch along the Malvern Hills. Soon Severn End with its impressive group of brick and timber framed buildings topped by tall chimneys is seen. This is the Lechmere family home. The earliest house was built by Richard Lechmere in the fifteenth century but much altered in later years. The house we see from a distance is seventeenth century although it sustained serious damage in a fire of 1896.

For some time now your attention may have been taken by one of the sights of the river, the white castellated building that rises above Cliff Wood. A romantic dream of a place, alas I can only report that this is Severn Bank, circa 1800.

As you draw near Cliff Wood the Severn Way continues beyond a metal gate. DO NOT PASS THROUGH THE GATE but bear right keeping the field boundary to your left. In 500 yards soon after passing Day House cottages bear left over a culverted ditch and right to join a wide track. After keeping with this for half a mile, passing Ryall's Court and a large pond, a metal gate is met. The bridleway continues as a grassy track but our route swings half right to cross a ditch by a waymarked bridge. Now head half left over the fields in the general direction of the Pepperpot to pass under the road to retrace your steps to your starting point.

8f: Severn Stoke and Croome Park

Starting: Severn Stoke, on the A38, 6 miles south of Worcester. It may be possible to park in Birch Lane.

Distance: 6 miles

Map: 1.50,000 Landranger 150 Worcester, The Malverns

1.25,000 Explorer 190 (was 14) Malvern Hills, Bredon Hill

NOTES: The National Trust has produced an illustrated leaflet which includes the public footpaths that cross the Croome Park landscaped area. Those looking for a shorter walk will find this very useful. Deer are present in the area - tracks suggest both roe and fallow.

SEVERN STOKE

Severn Stoke is an attractive village on the Severn Way and a good launching point for riverside walks. In the Commonwealth period following the end of the Civil War the priest was shot whilst in the pulpit by John Somers. In 1671 The Levellers, a radical political movement, had a base in the village and caused something of an upset in the locality.

We are, in this section, primarily concerned with CROOME PARK. The National Trust acquired the land in 1996 (but not the house - Croome Court - which is a private residence with no public access). The landscaped parkland had fallen into a sad state but the Trust with its usual energy and expertise embarked on a ten year restoration plan to give greater access to the many features of interest.

CROOME PARK was the home of the Earls of Coventry and who at one time owned some 50,000 acres in Worcestershire. It was the sixth earl who, employing the leading luminaries in architecture and landscaping, created Croome Park. It was the era of the grand design with carefully landscaped and extensive parkland where sometimes exotic cattle and sheep grazed, enhancing the idyllic views from the windows of the great house. Deer parks were added but not every thought was on the world of today. Estate churches, virtually private chapels, were built which over the years accumulated often ostentatious monuments to the dear departed with equally extravagant praise of their virtues.

Map 8f

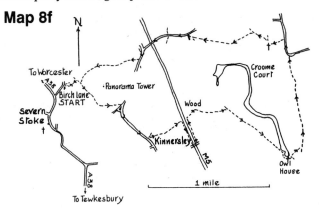

Here at Croome D'aboit the earl put heart, mind and soul, to saying nothing of his fortune, into the enterprise. It is tempting to regard this as keeping up with the Joneses or going just one better - the earl capped the lot and I for one look forward to enjoying the fruits of his restored dream. Fine trees were planted, ponds were sunk, an artificial river created and scarcely anywhere are there so many temples and towers, greenhouses, grottoes and grand entrance gates than here. Amongst those commissioned were Lancelot "Capability" Brown, Robert Adam and James Wyatt, famous names all.

The house built in 1751 of Bath stone, with square towers at each corner, and only seen from a distance, is attributed to Brown. The church of St. Mary Magdalene is now in the care of the Churches Conservation Trust which is also carrying out restoration work. It seems to have been a joint enterprise with Brown contributing the exterior and Adam the interior decoration. Within are a number of memorials to the Coventry family, including Thomas (1578-1640), a lawyer who became Attorney General and Lord Keeper of the Great Seal. He was a royalist and lent Charles I the then huge sum of ten thousand pounds. A descendant, Sir John Coventry, was to get into trouble when he made references to Charles II's association with Nell Gwyne, in the House of Commons. He was attacked and dragged from his coach and his nose cut to the bone.

One monument that was intended for the church is missing - a huge work commemorating the Earl who died in 1699. He had married for a second time rather late in life. The union was not well received for his bride was thought to be of humble birth. When the old earl died his son, the second earl, refused to have the monument placed in the church at Croome. It eventually found a home at St. Mary's, Elmley Castle.

THE WALK
Head up Birch Lane and as it curves to the left take the footpath on the right. (The map shows this crossing a grassy field half right and then over a small stream and forward along the wood edge.) It seems evident, however, that it has become the custom to go directly ahead from the road then swing left along the field edge which is followed until the woodland falls back. From here head up the hillside, over a stile and forward. On your left will be seen

the Panorama Tower on Cubs Moor, the first of the many devices that are encountered, which grace Croome Park.

The way (no visible path) curves to meet the road by a triangular junction. Bear right, signed Kinnersley. In just over a quarter of a mile, and 20 yards short of a telephone box, take the path on the left, heading half right over a field. Continue over rough grassland with a pond to your left, to emerge into an open field. Here the construction of the M5 has resulted in a slightly tedious diversion which defies common sense. Take the shortest route over the field to meet the M5 (the path is usually restored after ploughing and should be clear on the ground). It runs north-east then swings right to follow the field boundary to cross the M5 by the farm bridge. From the bridge turn left along the field margin. A little way into the next field head half right towards wooden fencing seen where Menagerie Wood meets a long narrow strip of woodland.

Pass through the gap between the two (a National Trust boundary board is here) and turn right on the outside edge of the woodland. Forward right you will see the church on the high ground that commands a view of the park. Cross a narrow enclosed green area, and go over a lane to a kissing gate and take the path that runs half right over a large field (two fields, strictly speaking). Croome Court, well away to your left, is gradually unveiled in its English Country House splendour. (When last I crossed this field it was growing a healthy crop of turnips - this would have delighted William Cobbett for when visiting Worcestershire in 1826 during the course of his famous "Rural Rides" he heaped much praise on the county's agriculture - his only mild criticism was a comment on the lack of turnips.)

Leave by a stile to find a view down part of the mile long Croome River created by Capability Brown. Continue to cross a weir and keep ahead on a narrow path. Soon bear left, signed Permitted Path to the Owl House. The building by Robert Adam was restored in 1986. Originally it would have had a full view of Croome Court and the river but the prospect has been partly occluded by subsequent natural growth.

Continue behind the Owl House, through a small plantation with a boundary to your right to emerge into the open. Remain with the fenceline for a further 100 yards or so. Here swing left towards the long line of oaks. Now a very different scene is revealed, not eighteenth century artistry but twentieth century technology, each with their own particular elegance. Here is as good a view as you are likely to get of the Defence Research Establishment at Defford with its satellite dishes, communication towers and row of great white golf balls in assorted sizes. It has almost a fairground look about it - a ferris wheel, perhaps a helter-skelter, the small dark buildings may house the ghost train and surely within the white spheres wall of death motor cyclists rev their engines.

Continue with the line of mature oaks and forward with the grassy track giving way to concrete and on to meet the road close to the tall arched gateway and lodge house. Bear left with the road, and in 200 yards take the path on the left which leads to the church. (A note on the stile indicates where the church key may be obtained in the event that it is not open.) The church site offers a view over the estate which includes the northern aspect of the house.

Emerging from the church swing right to follow the hedgerow, and bearing left on the falling path which runs to the right of a strip of woodland. Continue skirting the wood at the bottom of the field and onward along the next field to reach a reedy pond. Hidden away in the woodland is the Temple Greenhouse and the Druid statue.

From the pond cross the field towards a red brick house. On reaching the road at High Green, go ahead passing the Croome Estate Office with the Coventry Coat of Arms set in a wall. Cross the motorway bridge and continue at a junction signed Kinnersley. In a short distance by a further lodge bear right over a five-barred gate. Currently this is neither signed nor waymarked. Cross the large field, roughly westwards and passing the tip of a pond to reach a signed stile. Follow the outside edge of woodland which conceals a long thin lake. Bear right with the woodland edge, then left along the field edge and right over the stream to return to your starting point.

9
Bredon Hill

After the Malvern Hills you may feel that nothing remains to surpass their heady heights. Not so. This is the moment to introduce Bredon Hill. At the outset it must be said that the walker has to work harder to enjoy its many favours but the rewards are more than worth the effort. Here too you may feel that you have turned the clock back rather more than on the sometimes slightly crowded Malvern summits. Both have a rich bill of fare but drawn from different menus. The Malverns announce their charms for all to see in its shapely silhouette; Bredon is more demure, its lower slopes concealing the upper part - a broad plateau over 950 feet high that facilitates many permutations of route.

Much of Bredon is down to sheep pasture interspersed with woodland but the southern slopes have considerable areas under cultivation. A well-used bridleway which descends to Overbury passes through some good parkland. The planting of Scots pines in small clumps or to line two of the bridleways has greatly enhanced the landscape in the area of Lalu Farm. Bredon has two forts: the much visited summit Iron Age settlement that looks out over the Vale of Evesham and a smaller fort above Conderton on the south side of the hill. John Noake, the Worcestershire historian, refers to a cave on the hill. Lined with rocks it was believed to have been used as an ancient granary - apparently for the fort dwellers. Noake never had the opportunity to inspect the cave for himself - when he wrote of it in the mid nineteenth century it had already disappeared under a landslip.

Other features of the hill include the King and Queen Stone above Westmancote, held to have powers of healing by those with sufficient faith to walk round them three times. The stubby tower on the hillfort was built in the eighteenth century by Mr. Parsons, the owner of Kemerton Court. Bells Castle (private property) on a lane above Kemerton was the creation of the eccentric Captain Bell who died at the rope's end. He is said to have been a smuggler who maintained two French ladies there in considerable secrecy. A real

143

Parsons' Folly, Bredon Hill

castle, the seat of the Earl of Warwick stood on the high mound (private land) that overlooks the village of Elmley Castle on the north side of the hill.

Ranged around the whale-back bulk of Bredon Hill are a number of small villages all with footpaths that give access to Bredon and its subsidiary hills. Bredon with its church and great barn and Elmley Castle with a particularly interesting church and sundials repay a leisurely exploration.

Elmley Castle is perhaps the most commonly used route. From here the Wychavon Way follows the eastern side, with a diversion to the hill-fort, before descending to Ashton under Hill. On the north side a direct but steep path from Great Comberton will take you to the fort in exactly 1 mile. Another short but steep way to the summit begins where the lane ends at Woollas Hall Farm. William Cobbett, during the course of his "Rural Rides" (1826), stayed at Woollas Hall, describing the view he writes of the Malvern Hills as those "curious bubblings up". Looking out over Worcestershire and the neighbouring counties he opines that the agricultural scene is amongst the richest spots in England and becoming more expansive adds his conviction that there was not a richer place anywhere in the world.

Westmancote, Kemerton, Overbury, Overton and Beckford, which has a silk printing factory, all offer opportunities for walkers to select individual routes from the map in addition to Bredon's Norton and Ashton under Hill which are featured in the detailed routes that follow.

9a: Bredon Hill - The Iron Age Fort

Starting Point:	Bredon's Norton, off the B4080 Tewkesbury/Pershore road. No formal car parking.
Distance:	6 miles
Map:	1.50,000 Landranger 150 Worcester, The Malverns
	1.25,000 Explorer 190 (was 14) Malvern Hills, Bredon Hill

NOTES: This is a strenuous walk on good, easy to follow tracks with extensive views throughout which are rewarding at all seasons.
Roe deer and hares may be seen. This is a sheep grazing area.

BREDON'S NORTON is a small compact village clustered round the 700 year old church of St. Giles. The fine gabled and dormer windowed Manor House is late sixteenth century whilst Norbury Park was built about 1830.

Map 9a

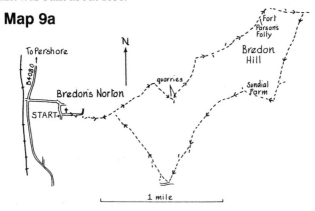

THE WALK

Finding a suitable and considerate place to park is a small problem which must be left to the walker to solve at his discretion. To get started on the walk take the village road that passes the path to the church entrance on your left (see sketch map). At a bend in the road bear right on the bridleway signed Bredon Hill 1 mile, soon passing the Manor House to your left. In a short distance leave the hard track to pass through a metal gate and head half right up the hillside, soon on a clear track. The waymarked and sometimes winding bridleway climbs through a succession of gates with improving views. They include the giant white golf ball satellite stations of the Defence Establishment at Defford, Worcester, if the day is clear, and brief snatches of the River Avon.

Your line of travel is steadily north-east for just over half a mile until the bridleway swings right through scrubland - festooned with Travellers Joy in autumn and winter - and an area of old quarries. A junction of paths is met in 300 yards - turn left. (Note there is a very good viewpoint from the top of an old quarry.)

In a short distance pass through a gate and swing right rising along the boundary fence over open pasture. Beyond a further gate continue on the outside edge of woodland to a stile/gate to bear right following a path through the long strip of woodland known as The Warren. (Roe deer may be seen in this area.) A gap in the trees near the point where the Woollas Hall path is met provides a window to the green fields of the Vale of Evesham and to Pershore with its tall abbey tower.

Keep ahead under trees, shortly emerging into the open and on to enter the Iron Age hillfort.

Sheep graze within the earthen walls, much as they must have done when they were brought into the compound when raiding parties threatened. There was no call for earthworks on the north-western aspect for the cliffs here are steep enough to dishearten even the most determined attacker - nevertheless the evidence of the slaughter of over fifty of the defenders shows that the site was not impregnable.

In the eighteenth century a certain resident of Kemerton built the tower which carries his name - Parson's Folly - now heavily decorated with the aerials of mobile telephone companies. Below the tower is a large, now broken, boulder known as the Banbury Stone around which visitors to the fort have laid out their own patterns or messages in stone. It's never the same display - newly arrived creative minds robbing previous constructions to make their own images of varying degrees of competence.

The views from here are even finer, the Vale of Evesham spread out below with map like precision, pasture, arable, woodland backed by distant hills. Pershore is easily picked out and the intermittent blue line of the Avon meandering through the green velvet of the fields. Immediately below the fort rough scrubby pasture is dotted with sheep - like distant yachts upon an ocean of green. The ubiquitous Malvern Hills provide one horizon and further away Shropshire's Clee Hills can be seen. Worcester too may be identified, the high rise flats of St. John's standing out in competition with the towers and spires of the city's cathedral and churches. Southwards Cleeve Hill is signalled by its wireless masts on the long Cotswolds scarp which will be in view during the return leg of the walk.

From the folly continue through the fort with the stone wall to your left. Ignore the small gate which admits the path that has climbed from Great Comberton. Make for the clump of pines seen ahead. Do not go through the gate but swing right keeping the boundary to your left as you edge several fields. A communications mast and Lalu Farm will be seen hidden in the trees with the Cotswolds becoming more prominent as you head south.

Partway down the fourth field keep ahead as your way is joined by a rough track. At the end of the field go through a gate and turn right on the path alongside the hedge which in 400 yards will bring you to the neatly restored Sundial Farm. The tree crowned May Hill above Newent is added to the scene.

Beyond the barn swing left soon passing through a gateway keeping the field boundary to the right. Continue beyond a large ash tree. A further gate is reached and the land falls sharply between a cleft in the hills. The way lies on a slight right diagonal soon following a broken line of hawthorn to reach and follow the inside edge of a small plantation.

As you emerge from the wood two paths are seen. Ignore the one that follows the left boundary and descend at an angle (perhaps between wire fences although these may only be temporary) and on through a deepening hollow way which must be at least as old as the hillfort. This path from the wood exit is followed for 600 yards until the rough lane becomes metalled.

At this point turn right through a green metal gate crossing a short field with a crumbling 'cliff' a little to your right.

At the end of the field bear right up the slope and take the forward left of two openings and keep forward with a hedge to your right. At the end of the field, keep ahead but now with the hedge to your left.

Maintain your direction along the outside edge of Aldwick Wood. As this comes to an end leave by a metal gate set a short distance down the field. Cross the field towards the tall ash tree at the end of a strip of woodland - heading towards Bredon's Northon. Keep forward over planks to make for the crest of the ridge with the roof of Norbury Park seen ahead. Bear left on the grassy track, through a gate and half right to leave by a metal gate and ahead retracing the steps of your outward journey to your starting point.

9b: Bredon Hill from Ashton under Hill

Starting Point:	The church, Ashton under Hill - parking may be possible by the sports field.
Distance:	7 miles
Map:	1.50,000 Landranger 150 Worcester, The Malverns
	1.25,000 Explorer 190 (was 14) Malvern Hills, Bredon Hill

NOTES: Another Bredon Hill walk with superb views. Initially there is a long ascent. This is sheep country, deer may be seen and buzzards soar overhead. This route does not visit the hill fort but an extension is possible.

ASHTON UNDER HILL is a pleasant village at the south-eastern corner of Bredon Hill, on the route of the Wychavon Way. The slightly straggling village is an attractive mix of timber framing topped by thatch, mellowed red brick and tile and an occasional stone house. There is a hint of the Cotswolds here - the more so when the excellent houses of Overbury are met on the return. This impression is heightened by the drystone walls that divide some of the fields. The small local quarries ceased to operate long ago and nature has reclaimed its own.

Look back as you climb on the outward route to enjoy the extensive views of the Cotswolds, Broadway Tower may be picked out as will Cleeve Hill. Slightly interrupting the line are the other Cotswold outliers - Dumbleton, Oxenton and Nottingham Hills, all over the border in Gloucestershire. In the northern arc the Vale of Evesham is spread before you with the Abbey Gatehouse built by the last prior easily picked out (north-east). In the south-west another tower may be seen, Tewkesbury Abbey, arguably the finest parish church in England. Nearer at hand a feature of the walk is the splendid grouping of Scots pines in the area of Lalu Farm, an inspired piece of landscaping.

THE WALK

The well waymarked Wychavon Way is followed from the start of the walk for almost 2 miles. We join it by the village church. Head through the lych-gate to the far end of the churchyard.

A smiling cherub looks down the path from the gravestone of Jane Dunn who dying in 1880 bequeathed £150 to purchase coals at Christmas for the aged poor of the parish for ever. Fellow feeling makes us wondrous kind for she was 86 when she died.

Beyond the churchyard and pond head slight right up the hillside to cross two stiles and bear right on a wide track. In about 100 yards take the path on the left and directly up the steep hillside. A waymarked post on the crest of the hill keeps you on course. Beyond a stile climb a bank and go forward over the next, level, field to a stile, and over the short side of an oblong field. From here turn half left (now with a retrospective view to the roofs of Ashton under Hill).

Beyond a stile bear half right to a metal gate and keep ahead on a grassy track. Cross a further track and go forward on the blue waymarked bridleway. Beyond a wooden gate bear right and soon bear left to follow a drystone wall to your

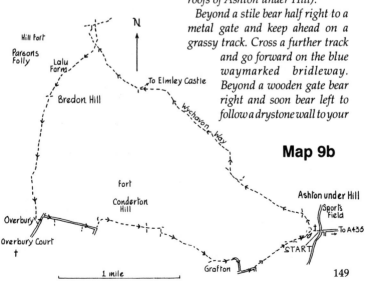

Map 9b

149

right. Remain with this (views to Evesham), later with Long Plantation on your right. In a mile the Wychavon Way is signed off through trees to the right and is abandoned at this point.

Continue on the outside edge of woodland passing the mast with its giant listening ears away to your left. About half a mile after leaving the Wychavon Way, as a path comes in from the right, turn left through a gateway and up the hillside. Continue beyond an old quarry to a gate and along a field edge with a line of beech trees to your right through which Parson's Folly Tower and the hillfort may be glimpsed.

The path descends to Lalu Farm with the groups of Scots pines to be enjoyed on the slope. From the farm head down the surfaced bridleway and over a crossing track to a gateway.

From here on there is a long descending way at first under trees then through fine parkland to meet the road at the northern edge of Overbury village in a mile. Overbury Court was the home of the distinguished founders of Martins Bank.

Turn left with the minor road and in 100 yards turn right to follow Pigeon Lane for about half a mile. When this swings right, bear left on a rough track, soon to meet a Y junction. Take the right fork and shortly bear right passing a barn on your left. Follow the good climbing track which lies under the slopes of Conderton Hill, where there is another hillfort, for 700 yards. Beyond a gate cross a north/south track and keep forward.

In 200 yards bear right to pass a barn on your left. Swing immediately left to a gateway, then forward over the field, passing a spring a little to your right, to meet a wooden gate. Pass through a thin belt of trees and bear slight right on a narrow tread to a stile with the hamlet of Grafton seen ahead. Descend the slope at a slight angle to a stile in a stone wall. Hold your direction to a small enclosed area and swing left with a wire fence to your right.

Exit by a five-barred gate and keep forward through Grafton, again a mix of stone, timber framing and thatch. At a T junction turn left by Middle Farm. In about 150 yards as the road bends right go ahead on a signed footpath. Head directly across the field, over a plank bridge and swing half left to follow the field edge with the tower of Ashton church coming into view.

A house and rough track is met. Cross this to a metal gate and on to the far right corner of the field. Follow the boundary on your right, passing a large pond with waterfowl, to reach a gate and return through the churchyard to your starting point.

West of the Severn

This section is a convenient pocket into which to pop several worthwhile walks which do not easily fall into other categories. Wooded hills are a strong feature and two walks are included which use part of the Worcestershire Way after it has left the Teme Valley. The SUCKLEY HILLS are part of a long tree covered ridge which runs north from beyond Malvern and rises again after the Teme has changed direction to push through a gap in the hills at Knightwick.

Those following the road south from Knightwick will find items of interest in the Suckley area. The White House near Suckley

Green Man at Holloways Heritage Garden Centre, Suckley

Green, built in Queen Anne's day, has a quite outstanding cherub and flower design over the door which you can't miss as you drive past. Just such an item might well feature at Holloways in Suckley village (near the church). Here is a real treasure trove of carefully selected old and new decorative garden items, which seen from the road defies anyone to pass it by.

Holloways were hop growers and their mouth-watering stock is sited in the old hop yard where the oasthouse and processing buildings remain. Amongst the hundreds of items for sale are figures of all descriptions, from cheeky little monkeys to demure but lightly draped young ladies, fountains, troughs, lead planters and pipe heads, meteorological equipment in the form of sundials and weathervanes topped not only with the traditional cockerel but by horses, dolphins and sporting dogs. Well-weathered stonework includes the mushrooms used to lift grain barns above the predations of rats, curved stones that might once have been round a large well or cider press and petrified oak.

OLD STORRIDGE AND BIRCHWOOD COMMONS which rise to a height of nearly 700 feet would hide a small army without difficulty. The walker exploring these areas will come upon attractive cottages tucked away in the woodland. Lower Tundridge Farmhouse near Longley Green with its impressively large timber framed construction is another eye catcher.

Further north on the Worcestershire Way the Abberley and Woodberry Hills look down over Great Witley with a double helping of treasure. WITLEY COURT, once one of the great stately homes of England, was partially destroyed by fire in 1937 and fell into severe dereliction. English Heritage came to the rescue, not to fully restore the house to the days of its greatest glory when royalty was entertained but to stabilise and repair essential elements of the structure - your imagination will do the rest. Within the grounds are two exceptionally fine fountains, which after much fundraising and work by the Poseidon Society are set to play again. The adjacent church, still in use, built by the Foley family, is a masterpiece of the baroque with fine painted windows, decorative plasterwork covered in gold leaf, mosaic tiling and an absolutely splendid painted ceiling. Do not miss either church or court.

Just a few miles away at WICHENFORD is a seventeenth

century dovecote (National Trust) with nesting boxes for over 550 birds. The nearby Wichenford Court is not normally open to the public but was reputed to be haunted. A long history of the house begins in the Saxon period but the alleged ghost refers to the early fifteenth century during the border wars with Owen Glendower. A party of Glendower's troops supported by French mercenaries raided the court. There are conflicting versions of the incident - one suggests that in defending her property the raider's leader was stabbed and killed by Lady Washbourne. A more earthy version suggests that a French noble who was assisting Glendower had been captured and was held prisoner in the house. Lord Washbourne being away at the time the lady made advances to the Frenchman who being a man of honour resisted her blandishments. Hell hath no fury like a woman scorned and he was fatally stabbed. The story of her haunting the bedchamber received considerable ornamentation with the haunting staged more like a scene from a classical ballet. Here she is alleged to be seen in a silver boat drawn by swans, and singing to a harp accompaniment.

10a: *Longley Green and Old Storridge*

Starting Point: Longley Green, 10 miles south-west of Worcester. Leave the A4103 taking the narrow lane from Storridge signed Birchwood.

Distance: 5 miles

Map: 1.50,000 Landranger 150 Worcester, The Malverns

       1.25,000 Explorer 204 Worcester & Droitwich Spa (Pathfinder 995 Bromyard).

NOTES: Another good autumn walk through rolling hill-country with fine views.

Reference has been made elsewhere to Worcestershire's hop growing industry. This walk gives some indication of how widespread the county's engagement in this crop once was. If you scan the landscape east and west from the high ground a number of the distinctive hop kiln chimneys will be seen. Batchcomb Farm, met in the early part of the route, was one. The present owner came here in 1950 and was still employing seasonal workers from the Birmingham area until

1976. It wasn't the dreaded wilt that led to a change but competition from eastern Europe. Heavy investment in mechanical processing was an option taken by some growers but this farm, in a sheltered valley between two high ridges, switched to fruit growing. Happily the kiln buildings remain to decorate the landscape with distinction although, like so many others in the region, they have now been converted to private residences. The first mile and a quarter of this route follows the Worcestershire Way with its black pear logo waymark. The return by the Leigh Brook includes part of the Knapp and Papermill nature reserve (Worcestershire Nature Conservation Trust).

THE WALK

From the village follow the road eastwards to cross the bridge over Cradley Brook and take the lane signed Birchwood. Ignore the first path but in 250 yards turn right on the signed bridleway and continue through the orchards of Batchcomb Farm.

At the farm swing left taking the tarmac road over the bridge. Turn right to a metal gate and head up the hillside. At the waymarked post turn to take in the view - a good photo opportunity if the light is right. Continue to the gateway climbing through woodland to reach the houses of Birchwood Common looking westwards to the atmospheric layering of successive ridges - a water-colourist's dream.

Turn right to follow the lane for a quarter of a mile. As the driveway to Birch Hall and the curiously named Anybody's Barn is met, leave the Worcestershire Way to cross a stile and swing left, (northwards) over a field to a gate with the views to the east now opening out.

Cross the next field to leave by a stile about 60 yards down from a gate. The retrospective view includes the mountainous aspect of the northern profile of the Malvern Hills with the Worcestershire Beacon looking particularly fine in silhouette. Head towards the house seen ahead. The climb to the 675 feet contour is now balanced by a long descent through the mixed woodland of Old Storridge Common. Houses are dotted here and there but you could have concealed a sizeable army here before modern technology left few hiding places.

Keep with the wide bridleway, which eventually becomes a tarmac lane, to pass Birchenhall Farm after half a mile. At a T junction bear right and in about 200 yards take the signed path on the left which swings right

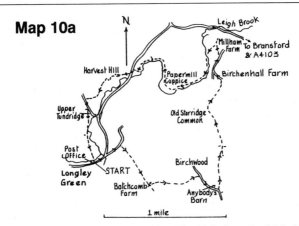

Map 10a

N

Leigh Brook

Millham Farm

To Bransford & A4103

Harvest Hill

Papermill Coppice

Birchenhall Farm

Upper Tundridge

Old Starridge Common

Post Office

Birchwood

Longley Green

START

Batchcomb Farm

Anybody's Barn

1 mile

towards Millham Farm. At the buildings bear left along the field edge soon to meet a metal gate to descend under trees and on with the Leigh Brook to your right. This is a more substantial stream than its name suggests and ought to provide good hunting for kingfishers although I was denied the pleasure of the quick flash of colour that is often all that is seen.

In a short distance turn right over a double-arched brick bridge and then swing left to follow the brook for almost a mile. At first along the edge of an open field then under the cover of Papermill Coppice with the stream digging a deeper bed for itself as you advance. At a division of paths do not take the left fork but keep ahead climbing to a gate high above the water. (Note the brook is attractively bridged near here and can be brought into use for future walks in tne area.)

Go ahead, through the field that is a green oasis between the wooded hills, to pass an old building and in 100 yards descend to follow the path under trees close to the brook.

After 350 yards emerge into the open continuing near the Leigh Brook for 400 yards. Exit by a stile and bear right up a steep bank then left to follow two sides of the field to reach the road.

Turn left towards Mousehole Bridge but before this is reached take the drive on the right - Catterall Farm on older maps but gateposts carry the legends Harvest Hill and Chase End. A little short of the houses turn left over a stile to cross two small fields then bear right along the fence and as you draw level with the houses swing left over the field to a stile.

Cross the next field soon on a slight right curve to a gate and on to meet and turn left on the lane. There is a fine group of buildings at Upper Tundridge. Here take the path found on the right (not the bridleway which is signed at the same point) and passing the buildings to your left, head over the long field with the Leigh Brook to your left once more. From the exit bear right for a few yards to a gate and stile then left along a wire fence over a large field. Cross a track, go over a stream and forward between houses to return to Longley Green by the village post office.

10b: Two Brooks Walk - Shrawley

Starting Point:	Shrawley Picnic Site - New Inn Lane. Location off B4196 2 miles north of Holt Heath
Distance:	9 miles or 2 miles
Map:	1.50,000 Landranger 150 Worcester, The Malverns
	1.25,000 Explorer 204 Worcester & Droitwich Spa (Pathfinder 974 Droitwich & 973 Great Witley).

NOTES: Muddy sections may be expected. The route is well waymarked.

This is a walk through varied terrain - conifer and broadleaved woodland, good striding bridlepaths, gently rolling grassland giving good views, a market garden, tranquil pools and almost secret ways along the hidden course of a brook to a mill. Heron are likely, many squirrels, kingfisher possible and watch for deer tracks.

Two brooks and a stream are followed during the course of this walk. All three were put to work at one time or another, with mills at Astley (not on our route) and Holt Mill on the Shrawley Brook. Dick Brook, a tributary of the Severn, is a narrow but deep bedded and swift flowing stream. In the mid-seventeenth century the brook was diverted to power a forge under the slopes of Upper Astley Wood, the scant remains of which may be noticed today. Further upstream a subsidiary river, the Nutnell, was also pressed into service to aid the operation of a small iron processing furnace. It is difficult today to visualise the Dick Brook as a navigable waterway but flash locks were installed during the time that the forges were in operation. The narrow and meandering character of the brook suggests that the craft being flushed downstream or given a little more depth to work their way the extra mile or so inland from the

Severn must have been very small indeed.

The man responsible for these enterprises was Andrew Yarranton (1616-1681) who started his working career as a draper's apprentice but developed considerable entrepreneurial skills. He drew up early plans for the Droitwich link to the Severn and to canalise the Stour. It is known that coal was being shipped to Kidderminster by 1665 more than a hundred years before the Staffordshire & Worcestershire Canal link with the Trent & Mersey was completed. Yarranton learnt the secrets of tin plate manufacture from the Germans and in agriculture he promoted clover as a valuable crop. Banking, inland waterways, the relief of poverty through proper employment, the development of the iron, wool, and linen industries as well as fisheries and a register of land ownership were all propounded by him but, alas, he was a man ahead of his time.

Map 10b

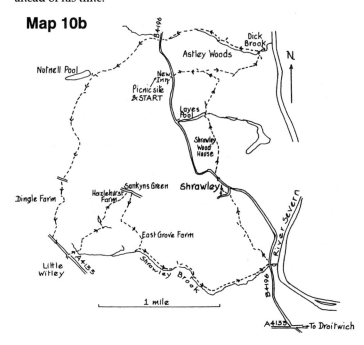

THE WALK

From the picnic site return to and cross the road following the, at first tarmac, bridleway soon to enter the Forestry Commission's Shrawley Wood. Paths make off in several directions but go ahead, keeping to the main track. In half a mile, after descending a gentle slope bear left with the bridleway. As you reach a steep slope at a Y junction bear left soon to reach and cross the Dick Brook by a small bridge.

Cross open ground to a stile and bear left with the fenced bridleway on the outside edge of Lower Astley Wood. Continue under trees and beyond a metal gate to emerge into the open now with Upper Astley Wood to your right. At a further metal gate bear half left over a field and over a second with Wood End Farm to your right, to meet the road B4196.

Turn left with the road. (Those opting for the shorter version of the walk should keep with the road to return to the picnic site). Once over the bridge take the bridleway on the right signed Private Road to Woolstan's Farm and Glasshampton Monastery.

About 150 yards after passing twin lodges leave the track, turning left over a small field to a woodland and ahead under conifers. In a few yards bear right on a track. In 100 yards leave it to go forward right on a narrower path to the edge of the wood and turn left. In 300 yards turn left back into the woods. (Note this is the second re-entry.) Go forward to cross a footbridge. In the next 150 yards there are a number of twists and turns - the general direction is south-west with the waymarked path leading into the open, facing Nutnell Pool.

Turn left with a bridleway into a large field. Head half right to a metal gate, then half left over a further field with conifer plantations seen ahead both left and right. Exit by a gate and continue along the neck of land between two blocks of woodland, passing a large deep pool to your left. At a gate go forward on a broad track soon with an orchard to your left and market garden crops to your right. As you near the road leeks give way to daffodils.

(The walk may be shortened by about three-quarters of a mile by turning left with the minor road to reach Sankyns Green in half a mile and picking up the route from the No Through Road.)

Cross the lane and go forward towards Dingle Farmhouse, with Woodberry Hill seen to your right. Just short of the farm leave the tarmac way joining the track to your left to bypass the residential area. Bear right with the track which shortly swings left to descend on a deep hollow lane before rising again to meet the Tenbury/Worcester Road by Primrose Cottage.

Turn left and in just over 300 yards take the path signed Sankyns Green found on the left opposite the turn to Little Witley. After a few yards of tarmac drive and beyond a gate bear right, descending to the Shrawley Brook. Very soggy ground here. After crossing two stiles turn left up the bank to a waymarked stile and forward with the boundary. As a pool is seen to your left swing right over a field then left along the hedge to reach a further pool and right along its bottom edge.

Head half left to pass the pond at Hazlehurst Farm. From the farm track the path is waymarked to the right corner of a large field to reach the road at Sankyns Green. Turn right and then shortly take the No Through Road on the right, a pleasant lane which is followed for half a mile to East Grove Farm.

Continue with the grassy path which descends towards the Shrawley Brook and turn left a little short of the footbridge. The brook runs in a deep narrow wooded valley with steep, almost cliff-like slopes. After a while the path is waymarked out of the wooded area. Here turn right along the edge of a field, thence back through woodland to cross a footbridge beyond which the paths divide. Keep forward soon with Holt Mill seen ahead - a fine building in an idyllic spot, you may think. Do not cross the brook but keep ahead on an improved path that briefly climbs high above the stream. When the way divides keep forward right, descending once again to the brook. Again, do not cross the brook and about 100 yards after the bridge head up the bank and swing right between a wire fence and trees.

After a brief passage under trees go forward to a stile to cross a long field to meet and turn left with the Stourport Road, B4196. In a few yards take the almost hidden path on the left and swing half right up the hill to a stile. From here take a half left to a gap in the hedge and swing right, passing under a pylon. At the end of the field dip down to a wet area where willows flourish and from the top of the bank go half right to the top corner of a field by Shotgrove Coppice.

Beyond a gate go forward to meet the road by Shrawley church, in red sandstone with box pews, minstrel gallery, funeral hatchments and a good royal coat of arms. Take the path through the churchyard and over a field half right to meet and turn left on the road. In 100 yards take the footpath on the right, passing a cottage, and on into woodland on a descending path. Bear left beyond a bridge, climbing on a hollow way then over a field to a *stile and gate with Shrawley Wood House to your left.*

Keep forward to a further stile and continue to the diagonally opposite corner of the field to leave via a gate/stile at Layes Pool. Keep the pool to your left and go ahead to the Forestry Commission board and paths in all directions. Take the narrower path on the right to follow the inside edge of the wood. In a quarter of a mile turn left and in a further quarter of a mile left again to follow the broad track with open country to your left which will return you to the road at the New Inn and your starting point.

10c: The Suckley Hills

Starting Point:	Longley Green - the village post office.
Distance:	5^1/$_2$ miles
Map:	1.50,000 Landranger (inconveniently on western edge of 150 and eastern edge of 149).
	1.25,000 Explorer 204 Worcester & Droitwich Spa (Pathfinder 995 Bromyard).

NOTES: This walk makes a return by the exceptionally well waymarked Worcestershire Way. Some other paths in the area do not appear very "user friendly" and waymarking is a bit sparse. However the Right of Way people have done sterling work throughout the county and it is hoped that all will be resolved. Watch waymarking for possible minor changes on the suggested route.

LONGLEY GREEN is another quiet village a little off the beaten track and lying to the south of the Suckley Hills. Two small curiosities may be mentioned. Stonehow Cottage of 1592 has a plaque too small to read from a distance which inevitably encourages the curious to make a closer examination. It reads "On this spot in 1765 nothing happened". The milepost opposite the Nelson Inn is unusually precise - "Worcester Cross 9 miles, Stocks ^{1}/$_2$ mile and 176 yards".

Springtime walkers will find the woodlands decorated with many wild flowers. As the season advances the list includes primroses, celandine, common dog violet from its deepest hue to white, wood anemone, dog's mercury, ramsons (wild garlic) and bluebells in profusion.

THE WALK

Join the signed bridleway by the village post office, descending on the Worcestershire Way to cross a stream and over a track to a metal gate. Bear left along the boundary to reach and enter a wood. Turn right with the Worcestershire Way but in a few yards leave it, taking the steep climbing path on the left which will bring you to a gate at the edge of the wood.

Here there is a fine view westwards over the long, wide valley -a rolling landscape which includes forests of hop poles set about with a web of twine, distant kiln chimneys glimmering in the sun, green baize pasture and Suckley church.

Follow the field edge northwards along the crest of Grove Hill. At the end of the field go through a metal gate with the bridleway descending diagonally left (not necessarily visible - there is a thick patch of broom across the slope) to the hunting gate at the foot of the wood. Go forward on the waymarked bridleway with the wood to your right. As the trees fall back keep ahead over the field, heading at a slight angle towards the valley bottom and leaving by a metal gate about 60 yards from the far boundary.

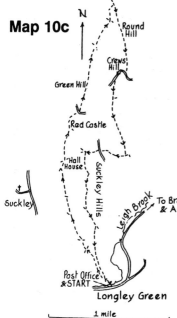

Bear right, following the hedge-row. As this falls back keep ahead to meet a gate and curve right between the two buildings at Hall House. Bear left to a gate, then forward for a few yards before heading half right up the long slope to exit about 60 yards from the top of the field. Go forward on a hedged way, passing the timber framed Red Castle and on to meet a lane by Steps Cottage.

Turn left and in a few yards take the path on the right and go left through a second gate and then over stile on the right. (For a short distance this follows part of a Worcestershire Way circular route.) Climb a steep bank to a gate and go forward with the boundary to your right following Green Hill northwards. More fine views include a closer prospect of the hop kilns by White House.

Keep ahead, ignoring the departure of the circular route as it turns left after 400 yards. When a wooden gate is met go forward through woodland. Continue with the boundary to your right to a further gate. Keep ahead over the next field, through a small wooded area and forward on the outside edge of woodland for about 300 yards. Thence continue into woodland, curving left to meet the signed and waymarked Worcestershire Way which is followed back to Longley Green, as described.

Fishhook back through the woodlands to start the return journey, following the waymarked path southwards over Round Hill for half a mile to meet a lane at Crews Hill. (Distant view here to Bredon Hill and the tips of the Malvern summits.) Turn right with the lane and in 150 yards continue with the Worcestershire Way as it takes the woodland path on the left. When it divides take the forward right path. The way broadens out, and when the right of way swings left keep ahead on a marked permissive path ie. about 600 yards from the lane.

In 500 yards swing right, rejoining the right of way, descending on a stony path to meet and cross the road. Go forward on a broad track with an orchard to your left to enter woodland. Ignore the first left turn but take the second, rising and falling. In half a mile bear left at a crossing path, descending on the bridleway to just short of the wood edge. (A window on the world here, with a view to Upper Tundridge and the hills.)

Turn right following the inside edge of the wood to meet a gate in 800 yards. Go forward with a hedge to your right, turning right at the bottom of a field over a track and stream and on past houses to return to your starting point by the post office.

10d: The Abberley Hills

Starting Point: The Manor Arms Inn, Abberley Village
Distance: 6 miles
Map: 1.50,000 Landranger 138 Kidderminster & Wyre Forest
                   1.25,000 Explorer 204 Worcester & Droitwich Spa
                   (Pathfinder 973 Great Witley).

NOTES: Superb views but steep ascents/descents make this a strenuous walk as it climbs through woodland to the 928 feet Flagstaff Hill.

The Abberley Hills from the Worcestershire Way

Abberley, lying under a long high wooded ridge, offers many walking opportunities from a good network of paths and quiet lanes threading through a rolling landscape. The Manor Arms is as colourful a public house as you may meet in a long day's march, for across its frontage are ranged the heraldic shields of no less than ten previous Lords of the Manor. Amongst them Pauncefoot, de Todenai, Beauchamp, Bromley, Walshe, Glyndwr and Jones. Jones? Yes. He was a Lancashire industrialist who purchased Abberley Hall, now a school. In commemorating his father, his son John, built one of Worcestershire's great landmarks - the magnificent clock tower that draws the eye from all points of the compass.

Across the way from the inn, and usually open, is St. Michael's, a towerless Norman church standing on a Saxon foundation. Following the dissolution of the monasteries - 1536-1540 - a dispossessed abbot, John Blamyre, was appointed Rector of Abberley by Henry VIII. He brought with him an unusual keepsake - the bell that had summoned his monks to the seven daily offices. The bell was hung in the nearby St. Mary's Church and continued to call the faithful to prayer for a further 236 years. Alas a crack brought an end

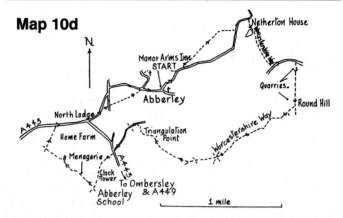

Map 10d

to its musical reminders. In the normal course of events it would have been melted down but it was saved and stands just inside the church door as a fitting memorial to both the Abbot and the craftsmanship of the bell founder.

One of the memorials is to Ann who married as her second husband George Walsh. Dying, aged 80 in 1679, she is described as "a person of extraordinary faith, high generosity and great charity mixed with extreme secrecy and modesty as if her left hand knew not what her right hand did...".

THE WALK

From the Manor Arms follow the lane signed Heightington for a quarter of a mile with views ahead to the Clent, Waseley and Lickey Hills. After passing the entrance to Crocketts Farm take the path on the left to the far top corner of the field and forward on the driveway to One Acre Cottage. Beyond the gate climb a bank, leaving the house to your right, and bear right with the hedgerow. Keep ahead over open ground and after skirting a boggy area (waymarked) resume your direction with a wood to the right.

At the end of the wood bear right over a small 'summit' on a diagonal course to the far left corner of the field to meet the road and turn left. In 300 yards (just short of Netherton House) join the Worcestershire Way, on your right passing a small lake with wildfowl. As the track bears left, keep ahead along the field edge to meet the road. Turn left and just beyond the quarry entrance at Shavers End take the bridleway on the right which continues under trees and with the aptly named Round Hill to your left. About 500 yards from the road turn sharp right to cross a field with a partial profile of the Worcestershire Beacon to the south.

Re-enter woodland on a climbing path. Ignore a path signed left after 200 yards and remain with the Worcestershire Way. (The route is so well waymarked - pear logo - on the long passage through the wood that despite a number of twists, turns and crossing paths detailed directions are probably superfluous.)

The path runs close to the wood edge with broken views to the south. As you reach the edge of the trees turn right, climbing with the great hole gouged out by the quarrymen largely hidden from view. At the top of this very steep rise turn left at a T junction now with a period of fairly level walking on a broad track. In about 250 yards turn right, soon curving left to resume your westerly direction. In 300 yards bear left with the path that joins from diagonal right, with veiled views towards Abberley.

There is a short dip at which point many paths meet. Veer right, climbing again before further level progress. Shortly after a path joins from the left bear right, soon with a slight descent on a narrow but still clear way. When a path is seen on your right that has climbed very steeply from The Hill, Abberley, bear left on a twisting climbing path. Following the crest of the hill with the slope falling sharply away to the right and a view south to Woodberry Hill. Later a wider window offers a better prospect with Abberley Hall and the clock tower seen below.

Shortly, a mile and three quarters after entering the woods at Shavers End the triangulation point at Flagstaff Wood, now adopted by the Bournville Walking Club, is met. From here follow the twisting descending path north-westerly to meet Wynniatts Lane in 300 yards by Brackenthwaite House.

Turn left with the lane which is followed for a quarter of a mile to meet and cross the busy A443. Continue on the stony surfaced track with the distant Clee Hills to your right and passing under the tall stone finger of the clock tower. (It seems to keep pretty good time - you may even have heard its chimes from Flagstaff Hill.)

As the school buildings are reached, leave the Worcestershire Way and turn right on the signed footpath, a wide track, soon passing The Menagerie Children's Farm. Here in the fields and pens are a varied collection of animals and fowl: a small herd of deer, donkeys, goats, chickens, geese and the like. The Menagerie is open during the summer from April for organised school parties and to the general public at various times including a Christmas event. It aims to present a "hands-on experience" for younger children. For further details contact Mrs Ballard, 01299 896704.

Continue past West Lodge. When the track bears right to Home Farm keep ahead on the path with a boundary to your right to reach a small plantation in 300 yards. Turn right with the trees to your left and cross into the next (left) field to resume your direction, north-easterly, to meet the road about 100 yards west of North Lodge.

Turn right and in 400 yards left, signed Cleobury Mortimer. In 300 yards take the tarmac path on the right. After crossing the road, go forward on a field path signed Abberley Village to reach a lane in 500 yards. Turn right to return to your starting point.

The Pegasus Fountain, Witley Court

The Cotswold Connection

Starting Point:	Fish Hill Picnic Site, off the A44, 1¹/₂ miles south-east of Broadway.
Distance:	6¹/₂ miles
Map:	1.50,000 Landranger 150 Worcester, The Malverns
	1.25,000 Outdoor Leisure 45 The Cotswolds (Pathfinder 1043).

NOTES: Excellent views but some steep sections.

Cotswold territory extends over more than one county with a small but particularly fine corner added to Worcestershire's scenic treasures, where the A44 snakes steeply down the strangely named Fish Hill to Broadway. Here is the classic use of the local stone, mellowed to dusty gold, with fine houses, a famous hotel - the Lygon Arms - and quality antique shops and galleries.

In this walk we are more concerned with the countryside through which the Cotswold Way passes, although our route treads a very small section. Wooded hills on the 1000 feet contour open out to provide extensive views over rolling sheep pasture dotted with fine houses and farms that mark past and present days of prosperity. Like the villages it is a well ordered landscape that will give much pleasure to the walker with a good path network offering opportunities for other outings that may be started from either Broadway or Fish Hill. Short waymarked circular routes - a Badger Trail and Woodland Walk - are signed from the picnic site.

THE WALK

Walk to the end of the car park and a hundred yards after passing the toposcope cross the busy road. Take the Cotswold Way into woodland, continuing through the hills and hollows of an old quarry, with orchids in season and views to Broadway and the wider world of Worcestershire. Continue to reach Broadway Tower. A notice here politely reminds walkers that they are now in the privately operated country park - keep to the footpaths but if wishing to share the park facilities and climb the tower, tickets should be obtained. We leave the Cotswold Way at this point, which makes a descent to Broadway.

James Wyatt was commissioned by the sixth Earl of Coventry to design the 65 feet high tower, an upmarket inland version of a lighthouse, you may think, and spacious enough once to have provided a holiday home for members of the Pre-Raphaelite group.

From the tower follow the marked route southwards to cross the track just inside the entrance gates to the park and leave by a stile opposite. Turn right with a quiet lane and in 400 yards take the path on the right. Cross the short field to a large firtree and stile - more good views. Bear left along the line of the wall to enter woodland by a stile in about 250 yards.

Keep forward for a few paces then turn right through mixed woodland, beech and larch, on a clear path. Curve right as an open area is reached, then over a crossing path to make a steepening descent under trees. At the foot of the hill bear right to join a wide track and pass the splendid Middle Hill House with its towering Cedar of Lebanon in its landscaped gardens. Bear left with the surfaced road and in about 150 yards leave it to join the track, right, passing the cottages on Knap Bank and continuing on a way lined

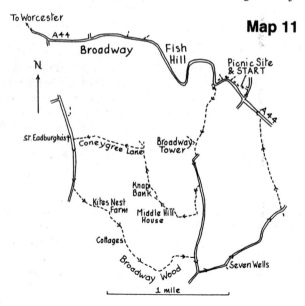

with more mature beeches.

Keep ahead as you leave the woodland to the cottage at The Lenches. At a gate and stile leave the main track as it bears right and cross the field towards a large tree. Now descend on the enclosed way known as Coneygree Lane, an old coach road, to reach St. Eadburgha's church in just over half a mile. The centre of the parish moved to the north, expanding round the Broadway we know today where a new church was built. The old is not entirely forgotten - open during the summer months it is worth visiting.

Turn left to follow the Snowshill Road with the hills ranged on either side. In 700 yards take the path on the left under the long avenue of poplars that will bring you to Kites Nest in 600 yards. Beyond the building curve right with the track climbing to reach Broadway Wood Cottages in a quarter of a mile. Take the grassy track beyond a gate, following the field boundaries with Middle Hill House away to the left adding architectural splendour to the landscape. Above it, like a giant ornate chess piece, is a glimpse of Broadway Tower. About 100 yards up the third field go forward on the wide track into Broadway Wood.

In 100 yards turn left at a T junction on a surfaced road. After 200 yards leave it to turn right on a wide climbing track under conifers. Keep ahead over a crossing path, still climbing. As you near the summit bear left for 50 yards then right to a gate into a lane.

There is a further longish spell of road walking here so if you wish to shorten the walk a little turn left and follow the lane passing Broadway Tower to return to your starting point in just under a mile.

Otherwise - turn right and in 200 yards left at a junction. Follow the single track road over the summit plateau for three-quarters of a mile, passing Seven Wells and Seven Wells Cottages. Take the footpath signed on the left that was the course of a Roman road, Ryknild Street, which ran from the Foss Way at Bourton on the Water via Alcester and Derby to South Yorkshire. There is little here to identify it as Roman except perhaps its straight course.

In three-quarters of a mile meet and turn left on the busy A44 to return to the picnic site in 300 yards.

12
The Vale of Evesham

The Vale of Evesham is well known for its orchards and market gardens. In 1725 Daniel Defoe described it as "that fruitful and plentiful country" but also mentions that the two largest towns, Pershore and Evesham were engaged in the manufacture of stockings. William Cobbett, writing a century later, was evidently of the same opinion for surveying the landscape from Bredon Hill valued it as "one of the richest spots in England".

Both Pershore and Evesham have strong monastic connections dating back to the early seventh century. Pershore Abbey in its day was one of the wealthiest in England. The surviving portion of the abbey is impressive - one could lose more than one village church within its confines. They built well, and not only the abbey for it was the monks who provided the fourteenth century bridge which still spans the Avon.

The Abbey Gardens at Evesham accommodates two interesting churches and the great gatehouse and clock tower built by the last head of the monastery, Prior Lichfield; it remains a landmark for many miles. Close by is the monument on the site of the high altar where Simon de Montfort was buried after the overwhelming defeat at the Battle of Evesham in 1265 in the Barons War. It is to him that we owe parliamentary democracy, albeit by a long and tortuous route. The abbey's almonery now houses the local museum whose treasures include a map of the world as the monks saw it in 1390 and a scale model of the town around the time of the dissolution of the monasteries.

Bredon Hill dominates the Vale. Here is the best of the walking country with rich rewards for the effort required to reach the summit. Chapter 9 is devoted to its exploration. The 40 mile Wychavon Way traverses the Vale from Church Lench in the north, crosses the Avon at Fladbury (picnic site at Jubilee Bridge), and on via Cropthorne to Elmley Castle, a delightful village, and the climb over Bredon Hill - a route that offers possibilities for planning your

Eckington Bridge and the River Avon

own round walks.

Winding through the Vale in a series of meanders is the River Avon - Shakespeare's Avon or the Warwickshire Avon as it is often called. It was improved for river transport from the earliest days of the canal age and now makes for fine leisure boating from the Severn at Tewkesbury through Worcestershire and on to Stratford-upon-Avon. The walker is not quite so well served as there is no continuous riverside path. Warwickshire has a 9 mile Avon Valley Walk from Stratford to the Worcestershire border - an extension onwards to connect with the Severn at Tewkesbury would be a useful addition to the national footpath network.

Convenient starting points for walks along the Avon include Eckington Wharf, by the six-arched sandstone bridge built in 1728, a successor to earlier timber bridges. From here the riverbank may be followed southwards for 2 miles to Strensham Lock where a lane leads to Eckington village. A picnic site on the A44 at Pershore Bridge allows access to a path on the north bank which may be followed for a mile and a half.

A corner of old Evesham

Evesham is enclosed on three sides by the Avon with riverside walks providing short excursions. North of the town there is a longer section of riverside path which is explored in the walk that follows. At Cleeve Prior a 2 mile stretch of the river may be followed downstream towards Billington Lock with a return made via Cleeve Hill. There are other short stretches of public footpath along the river but the lack of continuity combined with the long intervals between crossings needs to be taken into account when planning walks.

12a: Battle, Blossom and Boats

Starting Point: Merston Green long stay car park, Evesham

Distance: 5 miles

Map: 1.50,000 Landranger 150 Worcester, The Malverns

1.25,000 Explorer 205 Stratford-upon-Avon & Evesham (Pathfinder 1020 Vale of Evesham)

NOTES: Level walking on a figure of nine route.

Earlier walks have provided an aerial view of the Vale of Evesham from Bredon Hill. Closer at hand walking through vegetable fields may not be very exciting but orchards in full blossom - that's a very different prospect. This walk follows the river into orchard country, returning the same way. If a shorter stroll is required the Twyford Farm Picnic Site is recommended.

Heron, swans, Canada geese, and perhaps a cormorant will be seen along the river and from Easter onwards a steady procession of boats cruising between Tewkesbury and Stratford-upon-Avon.

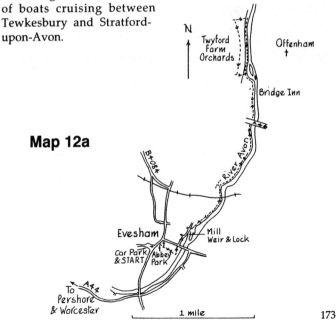

Map 12a

THE WALK

From the car park return to and cross the main road. Here is a corner of old Evesham - the Working Men's Club is fronted by the porch of the Abbot Lichfield Grammar School of 1514, later named Prince Henry's. The local museum is seen to your right, attractively housed in the Abbey's Almonery.

Make your way through Abbey Park, between the two churches which have some fine windows depicting the foundation of the Abbey following a miraculous vision and the Battle of Evesham. Carry on through the arch of the tower built by the last Abbot, Clement Lichfield, with a full peal of twelve and a carillon.

To the right will be seen the memorial to Simon de Montfort, buried under the high altar after the battle of 1265.

Descend to the riverbank and bear left to reach and cross Bridge Street then forward on Mill Street. As the road bends keep ahead passing factories to bear right in 100 yards on a signed path with a view of the mill, lock island with its steep pitched tent-shaped house and the roar of the weir.

Follow the towpath upstream, cross a slipway and briefly desert the river at a gate. Bear right soon to continue with the river. The Avon is wide here, busy with moorings, marinas and boatyards. Beyond the railway bridge it becomes more rural with willow and alder fringed banks and on the southern slopes, in spring, white misted orchards. Green Hill to your left was the scene of much of the fighting in 1265 when de Montfort and his Barons seeking to curb the power of the monarchy were roundly beaten by superior tactics and the tardy arrival of long expected reinforcements.

In three-quarters of a mile pass under the A46 road bridge, continuing with the village of Offenham seen over the river and the Bridge Inn at the old ferry site. About 100 yards after crossing a small stream a waymark post will be noted. Bear left here to skirt a substantial inlet. (Maybe a former docking place for the transport of the local produce?)

Continue upstream with the former railway line to your left, eventually meeting a strip of orchard. Half a mile from the ferry and when you are about opposite Court Farm turn left up the bank, and over the railway.

Go ahead on the surfaced track which edges the extensive modern orchards of Twyford Farm. In 200 yards turn left on a grassy track between the fruit trees. A modest height but with good views which include Cleeve Hill, Offenham with its market gardens, acres of glasshouses and the tip of its red and white banded maypole and the Cotswold escarpment.

In half a mile bear left to meet and cross the old railway line and make the return to Evesham via the riverbank.

174

13

Further Afield

Whilst we have contrived to provide a representative selection of walks throughout the county the possibilities for further walking are considerable. It is however time to look further afield for Worcestershire is close to other superb walking country and we have enjoyed the many scenic pleasures of neighbouring counties and the Welsh border country. The following is a brief description of some earlier titles.

THE SHROPSHIRE HILLS ISBN 1 85284 064 1
The hills of South Shropshire are a walker's paradise and in comparatively easy reach of many parts of the West Midlands. The book provides detailed routes over some of the finest territory in the area: the heather-clad Long Mynd, the rock-strewn mysterious Stiperstones, Croft Castle and one of the decisive battles of the Wars of the Roses, Bridgnorth and the superb view from High Rock, Caer Carodoc and some of the less visited but no less enjoyable hills around Church Stretton, The Clee Hills and more.

SEVERN WALKS ISBN 1 85284 164 8
We took the best part of a year exploring the riverbanks and countryside of Britain's longest river to compile a variety of walks each with a background commentary. From a peaty bog high on Plynlimon to a dizzy crossing of the Severn Bridge many aspects of the river are presented within the context of a rich scenic, cultural and historic heritage. The opening of The Severn Way in 1998 should make this book of particular interest to those unable to undertake the full 220 mile route.

WALKING OFFA'S DYKE PATH ISBN 1 85284 160 5
This is one of the great walking adventures of the border country as the 170 mile National Trail treads a path through magnificent scenery with a turbulent history. At first sight such a route may

seem impractical for those constrained by time or family commitments. Undertaken in its entirety the Trail offers an attractive and sometimes demanding prospect for the long distance walker. It becomes a promising possibility if taken in short sections, the walker can then spread his excursions over months or even years in day or weekend trips. Areas explored include the Wye Valley between Monmouth and Chepstow, the Hatterrall Ridge in the Black Mountains, the countryside around Kington, remote parts of Shropshire and the Clwyd Hills.

WALKING DOWN THE WYE ISBN 1 85284 105 2

Like the Severn the Wye rises on Plynlimon - only half a mile apart but the terrain dictates that they take very different courses with the Severn covering almost twice the distance before they are united just below the Severn Bridge. The 112 mile waymarked Wye Valley Walk explores fine riverside scenery and a landscape rich in history, from the engineering marvel of the Elan Reservoirs to the Norman stronghold of Chepstow Castle perched high above the river's tidal reaches. It visits bustling market towns like Hay-on-Wye, the country's second-hand book capital, the majesty of Hereford Cathedral; the romantic ruins of Tintern Abbey and the spectacular natural fortress of Yat Rock with its incomparable view of the river. Again the route can easily be split into day stages and enjoyed a section at a time.

14
Useful Information

TOURIST INFORMATION OFFICES
(note some may operate on a seasonal basis)

BEWDLEY: Bewdley Museum, Load Street, Bewdley.
Tel: 01299 404740

BROMSGROVE: Bromsgrove Museum, 26 Birmingham Road, Bromsgrove B61 0DD.
Tel: 01527 831809

DROITWICH SPA: St. Richard's House, Victoria Square, Droitwich WR9 8DS.
Tel: 01905 774312

EVESHAM: The Almonery, Abbey Gate, Evesham WR11 4BG
Tel: 01386 446944

KIDDERMINSTER: Severn Valley Railway Stn, Comberton Hill, Kidderminster DY10 1QX
Tel: 01562 829400

MALVERN: Winter Gardens Complex, Grange Road, Malvern WR14 3HB
Tel: 01684 892289

PERSHORE: 19 High Street, Pershore WR10 1AA
Tel: 01386 554262

REDDITCH: Civic Square, Alcester Street, Redditch B98 8AH
Tel: 01527 60806

UPTON UPON SEVERN: Pepperpot, Church St, Upton Upon Severn WR8 0HT
Tel: 01684 594200

WORCESTER: The Guildhall, High Street, Worcester WR1 2EY
Tel: 01905 726311

COUNTY COUNCIL SERVICES

RIGHTS OF
WAY DEPT:
Worcestershire County Council, County Hall, Spetchley Road, Worcester
Tel: 01905 766877 Obstructions - 01905 766876

PUBLIC
TRANSPORT
Timetable Enquiries (Bus) Tel: 0345 125436. Timetables available from County Hall, Libraries and Tourist Information Offices have local services. A Public Transport Map and Guide is published by the County Council.

Other enquiry points:

City of Birmingham area: Centro Bus & Rail Hotline Tel: 0121 200 2700

Midland Red West Buses Tel: 01905 763888

COUNTRYSIDE SERVICES
Tel: 01905 763763

COUNTRY PARKS, ACCESS & PICNIC SITES.

Ankerdine Common Picnic Site off A44. Access to Worcestershire Way.

Arrow Valley Country Park- off A4189 Redditch.

Avoncroft Picnic Site (by Avoncroft Museum of Buildings).

Blackstone Meadows - Country Park near Bewdley. Access to River Severn.

Broadway Tower Country Park - private management - admission charge, various attractions include ascent of the famous tower. Easter- October.

Cleeve Prior Picnic Site: Access to River Avon and Cleeve Hill Nature Reserves.

***Clent Hills Country Park, Nimmings Car Park - Hagley Wood Lane via the A456.
Fine views and access to North Worcestershire Path.

Clerkenleap Picnic Site - A38 south of Worcester: Access to River Severn & Battlefield viewpoint.

Eckington Bridge Picnic Site - off B4080. Access to River Avon.

Elmley Castle Picnic Site - opposite village green. Access to Wychavon Way and Bredon Hill.

Eymore Wood, Trimpley. Private woodland with waymarked walks. Access to Worcestershire Way. GR 776793.

Fish Hill Picnic Site - off A44 above Broadway. Access to Cotswold Way.

Forhill Picnic Site. Access to North Worcestershire Path.

Great Witley Picnic site - off A443.

Hartlebury Castle Picnic Site.

*** Kingsford Country Park 3 miles north of Kidderminster town centre:
Woodland with access to Kinver Edge, North Worcestershire Path, Worcestershire Way and the Staffordshire Way.

Lickey Hills Country Park (City of Birmingham). Access to North Worcestershire Path.

Marribie Picnic Site - off A456.
Jubilee Bridge - B4024 between Fladbury & Cropthorne. Access to Wychavon Way and River Avon.

Leapgate Country Park, Hartlebury Common Nr. Stourport, off the B4195.
Sandy heathland.

Nature Reserves: Worcestershire Wildlife Trust, several reserves including woodlands open to the public - others may require permit. Enquiries Lower Smite Farm, Hindlip WR3 8SZ. Tel: 01905 754919

Pershore Picnic Site (Old Pershore Bridge - off A44). Access to River Avon.

Pixham Ferry - off B4424, 4 miles south of Worcester. Access to River Severn.

Seaford Lane Picnic Site - off B4082. Nr. Naunton Beauchamp.

Shell Ford Picnic Site 1 mile north of Himbleton. Access to Wych-avon Way.

Shrawley Picnic Site - near New Inn. Access to Shrawley Wood.

Stoke Bliss Picnic Site - B4214, GR 631630.

Tank Quarry, Malvern. Access to the Worcestershire Way and Malvern Hills.

Tardebigge Picnic Site, Close to Worcester & Birmingham Canal.

Trimpley Reservoir (Severn Trent Picnic Site). Access to Severnside walks, Severn and Eymore Wood. GR 774792.

Twyford Farm Picnic Site - A436 near Evesham.

Admission charge for Twyford Country Centre - various attractions and shops.

***Waseley Hills Country Park A491 - signed from Junction 4 M5. Various facilities and access to North Worcestershire Path.

Worcester Woods Country Park.

*** Information from Countryside Service at Waseley Hills. Tel: 01562 710025

(Further country parks and picnic sites are in the planning stage.)

LONG DISTANCE & REGIONAL FOOTPATHS
(see Introduction for brief details)

Worcestershire Way (free leaflet & accommodation guide from Environmental Services, Worcs CC, Tel: 01905 766476)

North Worcestershire Path

Wychavon Way

Severn Way

Monarchs Way

BRITISH WATERWAYS

Worcester & Birmingham Canal - Enquiries Lapworth, Tel: 01564 784634.

Staffordshire & Worcester Canal - Enquiries Norbury Junction Office,Tel: 01785 284253.

The Severn Navigation is controlled by British Waterways.

NAVIGATION TRUSTS - RIVER AVON

Lower Avon Navigation Trust, Mill Wharf, Pershore, Tel: 01386 552517.

Upper Avon Navigation Trust, Harvington. Evesham, Tel: 01386 870526.

PLACES OF INTEREST

(selection only)

(Opening times quoted as a general guide - you are recommended to check current times.)

AVONCROFT Museum of Historic Buildings, Bromsgrove.
Mar-Nov. Daily from 10.30 but not Mons April & Oct and not Mons and Fris Mar, & Nov.

BECKFORD
Hand painted silk factory and shop. Daily except Suns.

BEWDLEY
Fascinating local museum. Daily to end Oct. Opens 11am.
See also entry under Wyre Forest.
West Midlands Safari Park - Daily Apr-Oct from 10am.

BREDON BARN. National Trust 600 year old barn.
Apr-Nov, Wed, Thurs, Sat & Sun from 10am.

BREDON CHURCH

BRETFORTON FLEECE INN
A National Trust Inn, formerly a medieval farmhouse. Open during normal pub hours.

BROMSGROVE MUSEUM

Domestic, costume, history and industry.

Mons-Sats from 9.30am.

CROOME PARK

A major restoration project by the National Trust of the landscaped estate of the Earls of Coventry.

CROPTHORNE

St. Michael's Church - interesting monuments.

DROITWICH SPA Heritage Centre, St. Richard's House.

Local history and broadcasting connections. Mon-Sat 10am-4pm.

EVESHAM

Almonery Museum Mon-Sat from 10am. Sun from 2pm (or from 10am in Aug).

St. Lawrence and All Saints churches in Abbey Gardens. For historical connections - especially in stained glass. Daily.

FLADBURY

St. Michael's Church for De Montfort window and Throckmorton brass etc.

GREAT WITLEY

Do not on any account miss the superb baroque church. Open daily.

See also entry under Witley Court.

HANBURY HALL. National Trust. Stately home and gardens.

Apr-Sept Suns to Weds, 2 to 6pm. Oct 2pm to dusk.

HARTLEBURY CASTLE

County Museum Mar-Nov, Mon-Thurs from 10am. Fris & Suns from 2pm.

HARVINGTON HALL

Moated medieval manor house. Mar-Oct. From 11.30am. Not Mon, Fri, Sat.

HAWFORD DOVECOTE

National Trust. Apr-Oct from 9am.

LEIGH COURT BARN English Heritage

Impressive 600 year old Tithe barn built for Pershore Abbey.

Apr-Sept, Thurs-Sun from 10am.

MALVERN AREA

Malvern Hills Childrens Zoo. Daily from 10am.

Malvern Museum Abbey Gate. Daily Easter - Oct (but not Weds in school terms) from 10.30pm.

Holy Well, Wells Road, Malvern Wells. Daily.

St. Ann's Well, via 99 steps from Rosebank Gardens Malvern. Daily.

Three Counties Showground - various events throughout the year.

MIDDLE LITTLETON TITHE BARN National Trust

700 year old barn. Apr-Oct from 9am.

PERSHORE ABBEY

Open daily - magnificent church from one of the largest monastic foundations in England.

REDDITCH

Forge Needle Museum. Apr-Sept, Mon-Thurs from 11am. Sat-Sun from 2pm. Mid Feb-Mar, Oct-Nov, Mon-Thurs from 11am. Suns from 2pm.

RIVER TRIPS according to season - enquire locally.

River Avon - from Abbey Park Evesham.

River Severn - various operators: From Stourport, Upton upon Severn, Worcester.

SEVERN VALLEY RAILWAY

Operates between Kidderminster and Bridgnorth.

Timetable enquiries Bewdley Station. Tel: 01299 403816.

SHATTERFORD WILDLIFE SANCTUARY (Nr. Kidderminster).

Daily from 7.30 or 8am until dusk.

TENBURY WELLS

Local museum, Goss School. May to Sept (closed for lunch). Tues from 10.30 and 2.30. Sats 10-30 to 1pm. Suns & Bank Hols from 2.30pm.

UPTON UPON SEVERN

Heritage Centre - The Pepperpot. Local and Civil War interest. Mon-Fri & Suns from 2pm. Sats from 10.30am.

Tudor House, Church St. Museum and garden - daily Apr- Oct

from 2pm.

WYRE FOREST VISITOR CENTRE Callow Hill Bewdley.
Daily from 10am with forest walks and facilities.

WICHENFORD DOVECOTE. National Trust.
Apr-Oct from 9am.

WITLEY COURT - GREAT WITLEY (English Heritage)
Substantial ruins of a great house with its fountains being restored and due to be working again from 1999. Daily but not some Mons. See also entry under Great Witley.

WORCESTER
Cathedral. Daily.

City Museum. Permanent and touring exhibitions. Daily except Thurs & Suns.

Commandery Civil War Centre. Mon-Sat from 10am. Suns from 1.30pm.

Elgar's Birthplace, Lower Broadheath. Daily except Weds and closed mid-Jan to mid-Feb.

Jan-Apr and Oct-Dec from 1.30pm. May-Sept from 10.30.

Local Life Museum - Friar Street. Two centuries of everyday and not so everyday Worcester.

Royal Worcester Porcelain - museum, shops, visitor centre and tours. Factory tours may require advance booking - Tel: 01905 23221.

OTHER CICERONE BOOKS BY DAVID HUNTER

WALKING OFFA'S DYKE PATH

Offa's Dyke was constructed by the powerful King of Mercia in the late eighth century to mark out the western boundary of his kingdom. Hundreds of years later this is the inspiration for a 170 mile long distance footpath traversing the border country of England and Wales.

David Hunter describes the whole route and makes suggestions for circular walks covering sections of it.

ISBN 1 85284 160 5 224pp £8.99

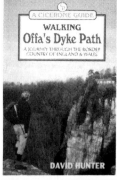

WALKING DOWN THE WYE

The 112 mile walk from Rhayader to Chepstow explores fine riverside scenery and a landscape rich in history from the engineering marvel of the Elan Reservoirs to the Norman stronghold of Chepstow Castle, perched high above the river's tidal reaches. On its way it visits bustling market towns like Hay-on-Wye, the country's second-hand book capital, the majesty of Hereford Cathedral, the romantic ruins of Tintern Abbey and the spectacular natural fortress of Yat Rock. The route can easily be broken into day stages and enjoyed one section at a time. David Hunters's keen eye for detail ensures you won't miss the many points of interest en route - and also makes enjoyable armchair travel!

ISBN 1 85284 105 2 192pp £6.99

SEVERN WALKS

28 circular half and full day walks based on Britain's longest river from its source to the sea.

Walks in the Welsh section include a trek to its source high on Plynlimon, following the Montgomery Canal to Powis Castle and a bird's eye view from the Breidden Hills. In Shropshire walks explore Ironbridge, Haughmond Hill and High Rock. The course through Worcestershire has much of interest around the river ports of Bewdley and Stourport, and the much tunneled sandstone at Bridgnorth and Redstone Rock Hermitage. Gloucestershire includes Tewkesbury, the Sharpness Canal and the Forest of Dean.

ISBN 1 85284 164 8 184pp £6.99

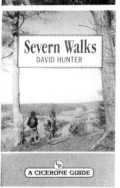

COTSWOLD BOOKS BY CICERONE PRESS

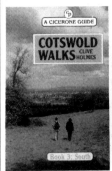

COTSWOLD WALKS   by Clive Holmes

The Cotswolds has much to commend it to the walker, being one of the country's major areas of Outstanding Natural Beauty, its numerous historical connections giving it an added dimension; indeed it is steeped in a history as rich and varied as anywhere in England.

The author has divided the Cotswolds into three parts and the 60 walks range from tiny Illmington in the north to Wiltshire's Castle Combe in the south. To the west the walks will take you to Stinchcombe within sight of the River Severn, whilst the area around Woodstock and Blenheim Palace in Oxfordshire is walked in the east.

Each book is profusely illustrated with finely detailed line illustrations. Clear instructions for each route are given together with an appropriate map. Further, each walk has a section titled 'Places and Points of Interest Along the Way' which gives an outline of history, local tales and anecdotes appertaining to the walk.

COTSWOLD WALKS BOOK 1: NORTH   *ISBN 1 85284 139 7   144pp   £4.99*
COTSWOLD WALKS BOOK 2: CENTRAL   *ISBN 1 85284 139 7   160pp   £4.99*
COTSWOLD WALKS BOOK 3: SOUTH   *ISBN 1 85284 139 7   144pp   £4.99*

THE COTSWOLD WAY   *Kev Reynolds*

A highly recommended practical guide to this popular walk, by one of Britain's best guide writers.

ISBN 1 85284 049 8   168pp   £6.99

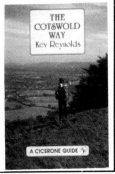

TWENTY COTSWOLD TOWNS by Clive Holmes

ISBN 1 85284 249 0 144pp
A4 landscape size
Casebound

Clive Holmes is an illustrator/author who has had a love affair with the Cotswolds for almost a quarter of a century: sketching , photographing and writing about its countryside, villages and hamlets.

In this book he concentrates on the towns and cities with their rich history and unique honey coloured architecture. The book, a rich mixture of anecdote and history, illustrated by the author's finely detailed pen and ink drawings and maps, will appeal to Cotswold residents and visitors alike.

The town described are: Bath, Bourton-on-the-Water, Bradford-on-Avon, Broadway, Burford, Cheltenham, Chipping Camden, Chipping Norton, Cirencester, Gloucester, Malmesbury, Minchinhampton, Moreton-in-th-Marsh, Painswick, Stow-on-the-Wold, Tetbury, Tewkesbury, Winchcombe, Woodstock, Wotton-under-Edge.

CICERONE PRESS have a large selection of guidebooks which cover most of Britain, many of the popular walking areas of Europe and worldwide. Below are listed some of the books in Wales, the Midlands Southern and South-western England

WALES

A WELSH COAST TO COAST WALK- Snowdonia to Gower *John Gillham* An ideal route for backpackers, away from waymarked trails. *ISBN 1 85284 218 0 152pp £7.99*

ASCENT OF SNOWDON *E.G. Rowland* The six paths to the summit. Revised. *ISBN 0 902363 13 1 32pp £1.99*

ANGLESEY COAST WALKS *Cecil Davies* Short, easy walks around the varied and historically interesting coast of the island. *ISBN 1 85284 266 0 104pp £6.99*

THE BRECON BEACONS *Davies and Whittaker* 33 routes described in detail with a commentary on everything seen along the way. Instructive and practical. *ISBN 1 85284 182 6 200pp £9.99*

HILL WALKING IN SNOWDONIA *Steve Ashton* Routes which appeal to today's hill walker, illustrated with many of Steve's exceptional photographs. *ISBN 1 85284 008 0 120pp £5.99*

HILLWALKING IN WALES Vol 1: Arans - Dovey Hills *ISBN 1 85284 081 1 256pp*
HILLWALKING IN WALES Vol 2: Ffestiniog - Tarrens *ISBN 1 85284 082 X 272pp*
Peter Hermon. A comprehensive alphabetical guide to all the mountains and lakes of Wales. *£7.99 each*

THE MOUNTAINS OF ENGLAND & WALES Vol.1: WALES *John and Anne Nuttall*
ISBN 1 85284 036 6 256pp PVC cover £10.99

THE RIDGES OF SNOWDONIA *Steve Ashton* Not just another guide! A mixture of descriptions, essays and photographs which convey the spirit of the route. *ISBN 0 902363 58 1 248pp £8.99*

SARN HELEN *Arthur Rylance & John Cantrell* The length of Wales in the footsteps of the Roman legions. *ISBN 1 85284 101 X 248pp £8.99*

SCRAMBLES IN SNOWDONIA *Steve Ashton* The classic rock ridges and other adventurous routes up challenging rocky faces. Second edition. *ISBN 1 85284 088 9 168pp PVC cover £9.99*

THE SHROPSHIRE WAY *Terry Marsh & Julie Meech* A circular route of 136 miles through some of England's finest counties. Hill country at its best, plus history in abundance from industrial Ironbridge to ancient Ludlow. Also described is the shorter Wild Edric's Way, 49 miles. *ISBN 1 85284 281 4 200pp £9.99*

SNOWDONIA WHITE WATER, SEA AND SURF - Canoe Guide *Terry Storry* The white water rivers, the coastal canoeing and surf beaches of North Wales. *ISBN 0 902363 77 8 160pp £5.99*

THE MIDLANDS

CANAL WALKS Vol 2 Midlands *Dennis Needham ISBN 1 85284 225 3 176pp £6.99*

THE GRAND UNION CANAL WALK *Clive Holmes* 13 easy stages along the canal which links the Black Country to London, through rural England. Delightful illustrations. *ISBN 1 85284 206 7 128pp £5.99*

AN OXBRIDGE WALK *J.A.Lyons* Over 100 miles linking the university cities of Oxford and Cambridge. Generally undemanding and easy to follow. *ISBN 1 85284 166 4 168pp £7.99*

WALKING IN OXFORDSHIRE *Leslie Tomlinson.* 36 walks from all parts of the county, and suitable for all the family. *ISBN 1 85284 244 X 200pp £9.99*

WALKING IN WARWICKSHIRE *Brian Conduit* Attractive pastoral and gentle hill walks include Shakespeare country, the Avon and the Stour. *Features many historic villages. ISBN 1 85284 255 5 136pp £6.99*

SOUTH OF ENGLAND

THE SOUTHERN COAST-TO-COAST WALK *Ray Quinlan* The equivalent of the popular northern walk. 283 miles from Weston-super-Mare to Dover. *ISBN 1 85284 117 6 200pp £6.99*

SOUTH WEST WAY - A Walker's Guide to the Coast Path
Vol.1 Minehead to Penzance *Martin Collins*
ISBN 1 85284 025 0 184pp PVC cover £8.99
Vol.2 Penzance to Poole *Martin Collins*
ISBN 1 85284 026 9 198pp PVC cover £8.99
Two volumes which cover the spectacular coastal path around Britain's south-west peninsula. Profusely illustrated. Full of practical detail.

THE THAMES PATH *Leigh Hatts* From the Thames Barrier to the source. *ISBN 1 85284 270 9 184pp £7.99*

THE TWO MOORS WAY *James Roberts* 100 miles crossing Dartmoor, the delightful villages of central Devon and Exmoor to the rugged coast at Lynmouth. *ISBN 1 85284 159 1 100pp £5.99*

THE WEALDWAY & THE VANGUARD WAY *Kev Reynolds* Two long distance walks in Kent, from the outskirts of London to the coast. *ISBN 0 902363 85 9 160pp £4.99*

CANAL WALKS Vol 3 South *Dennis Needham ISBN 1 85284 227 X 176pp £6.99*

WALKING IN THE CHILTERNS *Duncan Unsworth*
35 short circular walks in this area of woods and little valleys with cosy pubs and old churches. *ISBN 1 85284 127 3 184pp £6.99*

A WALKER'S GUIDE TO THE ISLE OF WIGHT *Martin Collins & Norman Birch* The best walks on this sunshine island, including short circuits and longer trails. *ISBN 1 85284 221 0 216pp £9.99*

THE SOUTH-WEST

WALKING IN CORNWALL *John Earle* Walks include the Coast Path, and the interesting interior. *ISBN 1 85284 217 2 200pp £9.99*

WALKING ON DARTMOOR *John Earle* The most comprehensive walking guide to the National Park. *ISBN 0 902363 84 0 224pp £6.99*

WALKING IN DEVON *David Woodthorpe* 16 coastal, 15 countryside and 14 Dartmoor walks. *ISBN 1 85284 223 7 200pp £9.99*

WALKING IN DORSET *James Roberts* Circular walks between 5 and 12 miles in a rich variety of scene. Spectacular coastline, lovely downs and fine pubs. *ISBN 1 85284 180 X 232pp £7.99*

A WALKER'S GUIDE TO THE PUBS OF DARTMOOR *Chris Wilson & Michael Bennie* 60 Dartmoor inns. Everything a walker needs to know. *ISBN 1 85284 115 X 152pp £5.99*

EXMOOR & THE QUANTOCKS *John Earle* Walks for all the family on the moors, valleys and coastline. *ISBN 1 85284 083 8 200pp £6.99*

WALKING IN SOMERSET *James Roberts* Walks between 3 and 12 miles, gentle rambles to strenuous hikes, on Exmoor, the Quantocks and the pastoral lowlands. *ISBN 1 85284 253 9 280pp £10.99*

CICERONE PRESS

A FULL CATALOGUE IS AVAILABLE FROM
Cicerone Press, 2 Police Square, Milnthorpe, Cumbria,
LA7 7PY. Tel: 015395 62069
E-mail: info@cicerone.demon.co.uk   Web Site:
www.cicerone.demon.co.uk